WHO BUT A WOMAN?

Beverly La Haye

WHO
BUT
A
WOMAN?

by

Beverly LaHaye

Thomas Nelson Publishers
Nashville • Camden • New York

Published in Nashville, Tennessee, by Thomas Nelson, Inc., and distributed in Canada by Lawson Falle, Ltd., Cambridge, Ontario.

Printed in the United States of America.

ISBN 0-8407-5946-0

Contents

WHO BUT A WOMAN?

Chapter 1

THE POWER OF
COURAGEOUS WOMEN

Never underestimate the power of a woman. Courageous women have been known to help save a nation.

Several years ago I read an account of what the women of Brazil did to save their nation from a communist takeover. I've been wanting to share it ever since then, because it shows so clearly what Christian women can accomplish if they will just work and pray together for a common cause.

In the early 1960s, the nation of Brazil teetered on the brink of communist revolution. The nation was ruled by morally corrupt men who allowed themselves to be manipulated by communist subversives. Inflation was rampant; government officials were regularly embezzling the hard-earned money of the peasants, and communist agents had nearly taken complete control of the government.

Alarmed by the spread of communism and political opportunism, several prominent businessmen began meeting informally in 1961 to halt Brazil's plunge into totalitarianism. Out of their meetings came an organization called the Institute for Economic and Social Research (IESR). The goal of this organization was to search for the cause of Brazil's social decline and then to present solutions. It began as an educational organization, but soon developed into an effective intelligence network as well.

The IESR sought to discover how Moscow's underground subversives were influencing Brazil's government policy and public opinion. Through its anticommunist agents, the IESR discovered that the Communists had wormed their way into high positions within the government, usually serving as second in command or as advisers to senior government officials. The minister of justice, the attorney general, the prime minister, and the press secretary to the president—all were dedicated communist subversives.

In preparation for the planned uprising, both Russian- and Chinese-trained Communists were stockpiling weapons, training Brazilians in guerrilla warfare, and developing "hit lists" of prominent anti-Communists.

In addition, the IESR found that the Ministry of Education was rife with Communists who were using literacy campaigns to teach the peasants Marxist doctrine. The children's readers in school contained blatant communist propaganda. Cooperating with the communist-controlled education department was the National Students Union, which was helping to carry on the literacy campaign as well as fomenting campus riots and terrorism.

The future of Brazil looked bleak. But the businessmen went to work to produce educational materials that exposed the communist plan for the takeover of their nation. Their pamphlets and exposés were distributed by the millions throughout Brazil—alerting the Brazilian populace to the imminent Marxist revolution.

These enterprising businessmen even established their

own television network of one hundred stations in an effort to overcome the censorship they encountered on the state-run stations. That educational effort was a monumental task. And yet their concerted campaign to tell the truth about communism finally defeated the Communists.

Who was responsible for the final defeat of the Communists in Brazil? These men gave credit to the women of Brazil! In "The Country That Saved Itself," (*Reader's Digest*, November 1964, pp. 135-158), author Clarence W. Hall made this statement:

> To the women of Brazil belongs a huge share of the credit for stopping the planned Red takeover. By the thousands, on a scale unmatched in Latin American history, housewives threw themselves into the struggle and, more than any other force, they alerted the country. "Without the women," says one leader of the counterrevolution, "we could never have halted Brazil's plunge toward communism. While many of our men's groups had to work undercover, the women could work in the open—and how they worked!"[1]

Leading the women against communism was fifty-nine-year-old Doña Amelia Bastos, the wife of a retired army doctor. After listening to her husband and friends discuss the serious problems facing Brazil, she gathered her own neighbors to her house one afternoon and challenged them: "Who has more at stake in what's happening to our country than we women?...Whose future but our children's and grandchildren's will disappear if the government's policies lead to communist conquest of our country?"[2]

Before the end of the day, she and her friends had organized the Campaign of Women for Democracy (CAMDE). Within a few weeks, she was establishing dozens of "cells" or chapters of women throughout the community.

Together, those concerned women of Brazil met in homes to pray and act. They organized protest meetings, and they purchased time on television and in newspapers and magazines to spread the truth about Communist subversion. They debated leftists and were instrumental in distributing millions of leaflets and booklets throughout Brazil!

In one instance, the women embarrassed and defeated a prominent Communist Party official who was planning on flying into the city of Belo Horizonte to give a speech. The women notified the Communist leaders that hundreds of women would be lying on the airfield when the plane was preparing to land. They thwarted the landing, and the speech was never given!

On another occasion, a Communist arrived at a hall to deliver a speech and was drowned out by the sound of rosary beads and the prayers of three thousand women. He, too, left without giving his speech.

As the women's movement gained strength, the leaders organized a massive "March of the Family with God toward Freedom" and filled the streets with over six hundred thousand women, marching and singing under anticommunist banners. During the festivities, the women made a public declaration:

This nation which God has given us, immense and marvelous as it is, is in extreme danger. We have allowed men of limitless ambition, without Christian faith or scruples, to bring our people misery, destroying our economy, disturbing our social peace, to create hate and despair. They have infiltrated our nation, our government administration, our armed forces and even our churches with servants of totalitarianism....[3]

Through the courageous actions and prayers of hundreds of thousands of women in Brazil, that nation was saved from a bloody Communist revolution! Who but a woman could have led such a successful educational campaign against Marxism?

Do you see the potential that the women of America have for bringing about a restoration of our nation to moral sanity?

I sincerely believe that God is calling the Christian women of America to draw together in a spirit of unity and purpose to protect the rights of the family. I believe it is time for us to set aside our doctrinal differences to work for a spiritually renewed America. Who but a woman is as deeply concerned about her children and her home? Who but a woman has the time, the intuition, and the drive to restore our nation?

The women of this nation are at a crossroads of history. The battle lines are becoming more clearly defined. The forces of darkness are becoming darker. There is no neutral ground in the battle to come.

As you will see in later chapters, some feminists are becoming more and more open about their true objectives: lesbianism, Marxism, and extreme social change. These are the radical feminists, the leaders of the movement whose objectives are much different from what some of their followers realize.

In Brazil, the subversives called themselves Communists; in America, they may call themselves feminists or humanists. The label makes little difference, because many of them are seeking the destruction of morality and human freedom.

You have a choice to make on this issue. The lines are clearly drawn. I hope this book will inspire you to take a stand.

Chapter 2

WHO BUT A WOMAN?

If you take an honest look at American history, you'll discover that women have often been in the forefront of social reform movements, especially ones that would strengthen and promote family stability. (You'll also discover that radicalized women have led some of the most morally corrupt organizations in America.)

American women have just as much at stake in protecting their families and their society from chaos as did the Brazilian women over two decades ago. Increasingly, American women have joined together in organizations that are geared to single issues. Some have formed or joined antiabortion groups, others are working with unwed mothers, prostitutes, drug addicts, or alcoholics.

The question I have often asked myself is this: Why have women been so conspicuous in these social reform movements? Someone once remarked that perhaps it is because God has implanted in a woman's heart and mind an aggressiveness that shows itself most obviously when her children or husband is threatened. Even in the animal kingdom, we see examples of lionesses fighting to the death to protect their offspring, and normally docile mother dogs will become vicious when they sense that their puppies are in danger.

I believe that God has deliberately designed males and

15

females to be different not only in their physiques, but also in the way they think, feel, and act. The woman has been gifted by God to bring life into the world. Deep within her spirit, she has a God-given mothering instinct, which seeks to protect and comfort those around her.

Even in our so-called "liberated" age, women still overwhelmingly choose occupations that can be viewed as extensions of the mothering role in the home. They become school teachers, nurses, doctors, dentists, dental assistants, and social workers. All of these are people-oriented fields; all are areas where a woman can provide comfort and service to those in need.

Women instinctively have this desire to protect, comfort, and serve. I am certain this is a major reason why they have been so aggressive in social reform movements. They see their families and lives coming under attack and they cannot remain passive.

Women Organize to Protect Lives!

In recent years, a number of women who hold to traditional values have formed grassroots organizations to solve serious social problems. Many of these women have become involved in protecting the family as a result of some terrible personal tragedy.

Candy Lightner is one such woman. Her teen-age daughter Cari was walking home along the road several years ago when a drunk driver plowed into her, crushing her body. She died in a coma several hours later. The driver never even stopped to help.

After Cari's tragic death, Candy learned that this drunk driver had previously been convicted, but had only been given a slap on the wrist. This time he killed a beautiful young girl. Candy Lightner began to demand justice against drunk drivers in California and decided to form an organization called Mothers Against Drunk Drivers (MADD).

Out of her personal anguish—and her desire to protect the lives of other children from drunks and lenient court judges—she now has a nationwide organization with MADD chapters in over forty states.

This one woman has been effective in getting drunk driving laws toughened up in one state after another since 1979. A drunk driving law, passed in Maine in 1981, for example, reduced the death rate by 41 percent in the first year. A MADD-promoted law in Florida resulted in a 50 percent increase in arrests and a 12 percent reduction in alcohol-related traffic deaths.

All over America women like Candy Lightner have become involved in forming MADD chapters. In September of 1982, for instance, an enraged grandmother in Alaska formed the first MADD chapter in that state. Mrs. June Gerrish became involved in MADD after her two grandsons were killed instantly by a drunk driver. Within three months after forming her chapter, she had enlisted the support of some three hundred people. Through the work of June Gerrish, Alaska now has one of the toughest drunk driver laws in America!

These women, and hundreds more, are working in their states to get swift and severe punishment for those who choose to drink and drive. They are saving hundreds of lives each year because they are willing to stand up for their beliefs!

Exposing the Humanistic Educational Establishment

Barbara Morris received a degree in pharmacy from

Rutgers University, but since 1969, she has devoted her considerable writing talents to exposing the secular humanist control of what has been misnamed "public education."

Since 1969, Mrs. Morris has written such books as *Change Agents in the Schools* and *Why Are You Losing Your Children?* to alert Christian parents to the dangers of the government educational system. In addition, she publishes a well-written and exhaustively detailed monthly report, *The Barbara Morris Report*, which keeps her readers up-to-date on the latest New Age and humanistic threats to our youngsters.

Mrs. Morris has used her God-given talent to benefit all who are concerned about the moral corruption in our schools. In one sense she is acting as an Old Testament prophet, warning the Christian community of the spiritual damage being done to our children. I have nothing but the utmost respect for her. We need thousands more like her.

Child Molesters and a Concerned Grandmother

Amy Sue Seitz was only two-and-a-half years old when Theodore Francis Frank kidnaped her. He raped her, tore off her nipples with vice grip pliers, and then strangled her to death. Her lifeless body was then dumped in a canyon.

Her grandmother, Patti Linebaugh, once told reporters, "When they told me that dogs had found her naked, mutilated body in a canyon and dragged it home, I made a vow that I would do something. I couldn't help Amy Sue, but I thought I might be able to help save others."

To keep the vow she had made, Patti Linebaugh

formed an organization known as Concerned Citizens for Stronger Legislation Against Child Molesters (SLAM). Through her grassroots organization, Mrs. Linebaugh is helping to set up SLAM chapters all over America. The purpose of SLAM? To get men like Theodore Frank behind bars—and to keep them there.

Theodore Frank is a pedophile, a man who enjoys having sex with little children. Just prior to murdering Amy Sue, Frank had been released as "cured" from a state hospital where he had spent four years undergoing rehabilitation. During his psychiatric treatment, Frank admitted to assaulting from 100 to 150 children over a twenty-year period. The California justice system had classified Frank as a mentally disordered sex offender who needed treatment, not a long jail sentence. Before arriving in California, Frank had spent time in a state hospital in St. Louis and a Missouri state prison as well.

SLAM is working for tougher sentencing for men like Theodore Frank. It is also pushing for changes in the way sexually abused children are treated during the investigation and sponsoring legislation which requires a criminal record check of anyone applying for a job involving children.

In California, SLAM was successful in getting a law passed that abolished the state's mentally disordered sex offender program. Men like Frank will be jailed, not pampered in treatment centers. The cruel death of one little girl sparked a national organization that is working to save other children from a similar fate.

Reaching Homosexuals

In Daisy Hepburn's book, *Why Doesn't Somebody Do Something* (a book which details the ministries of twenty different women), I read the inspiring story of Robbi Kenney, a young woman in Minneapolis who founded OUTPOST, a ministry to Christians who are struggling with their homosexuality. Kenney asks the question:

What is a twenty-five-year-old woman without a degree in counseling or administration, without formal Bible training, and without a gay testimony doing in a ministry like this?

I think God wanted to make a point, to show the church that believers who have never been gay can help someone who is. And He took a person without any previous understanding of the problem to show that all He needs to accomplish His will is for her to have a willing heart to serve Him, regardless of where that leads.[1]

Robbi Kenney first became involved in counseling homosexuals when she discovered that a young man she had known in high school had become a homosexual. She began to read everything she could find about homosexuality and sought advice from professional counselors and her pastor. Eventually she attended a conference in Anaheim on homosexuality.

She admits that during the early years of her ministry, she wasn't fully committed to working with homosexuals because she had always wanted to be involved in missions work. But the Lord kept steering her in the direction of work with homosexuals.

Today, OUTPOST is one of the most effective ministries to homosexuals in America. According to Kenney, her ministry is dedicated to three objectives:

1) Educating the church to its responsibility and capability of ministering to a group of people largely ignored due to the nature of their sin; 2) discipling believers in

such a way that they can walk in freedom given to them at salvation as new creatures in Christ, over all areas of sin, but particularly homosexuality; and 3) evangelizing the gay community with the Good News of Jesus Christ and the message of freedom from gayness possible to those who make Christ their Lord.[2]

Here is a young woman who rather reluctantly was drawn into a ministry to homosexuals but who has been transformed by the power of God into an articulate and effective leader. Through her ministry, thousands of homosexuals are finding hope and victory over their life-controlling sin. Robbi Kenney has been an effective tool for the Lord because she was willing to be used.

Fighting Child Pornography

Beverly Heinrich was rather naive about the extent of the problem of child pornography in Texas until after she had attended a meeting of community leaders who were alarmed over the increase in pornography in Houston.

Mrs. Heinrich was unaware of the nature and extent of pornography. She had never even seen a centerfold in *Playboy* magazine, let alone imagined the depravity that went on in peep show booths. She was soon to find out, however. During the meeting of concerned citizens, she was appointed to investigate the extent of the pornography problem and compile a report on the subject.

"I was shocked at what I saw, and then I couldn't communicate to anybody else what was happening without almost being as explicit as the movies themselves were," she said. "I found peep shows where people could go into a little four-by-four booth. They could watch a movie for a few dollars and they could have sexual conduct either by themselves or they could knock on the wall and have sexual conduct through a hole in the wall with the person in the next booth."[3]

She had never been concerned about the pornography plague threatening her home, but she soon discovered that women from all types of backgrounds, including prayer groups she visited, had been victimized by pornography. As she became more and more involved in investigating obscenity, many Christian women opened up to her and described the terrible lives they had been living. One woman she encountered had been an incest victim, and her father was a leader in a fine church.

After one prayer meeting, a young woman came up to Mrs. Heinrich and poured her heart out. Her ex-husband loved pornography and had spent years forcing her to submit to spankings as part of a cruel, sado-masochistic ritual. She was eventually covered with bruises from these beatings. The situation became far worse, however, when he began beating the children as well in order to achieve sexual gratification. She sought and obtained a divorce.

These and other equally alarming stories convinced Beverly Heinrich that she had to fight pornography, which was not a victimless crime as some claim. She was meeting victims everywhere she went. She soon began organizing antipornography rallies in Houston and finally went to the Texas legislature to urge passage of tough antipornography laws.

Her first attempts weren't successful, but her perseverance paid off. The governor commissioned a House Select Committee on Child Pornography to investigate the problem and make recommendations for legislative remedies. Beverly Heinrich became the chief researcher on this committee and spent nine months gathering materials on the extent of the pornography plague in Texas.

After six years of fighting pornography, Beverly Heinrich and her supporters managed to aid in the passage of two major antipornography laws and ten resolutions dealing with pornography. In addition, the Texas Department of Human Resources was required to reevaluate its program for sexually abused children in order to be more sensitive to their needs. In Houston, Beverly's activities were responsible for the formation of a vice squad on the police force to deal with obscenity and pornography.

Her fight against child pornography was not accomplished without sacrifice and fear on her part. During her battle to stop pornography, her car windshield was twice shattered by hoodlums; her car was egged and its tires slashed. Out of fear for her life, she put a huge fence around her backyard and bought a guard dog. But she didn't give up—and she has been successful.

Women on the Move

I could go on and on telling you stories of other women who have risked their reputations and even their lives to stand for righteousness against other social evils in our nation. But I think you understand what I am saying. These women, like their counterparts in Brazil, have found themselves threatened by a permissive society, by humanistic thinking, and by a legal system that often protects the guilty and punishes the innocent.

They have made a choice to oppose evil and have devoted years of their lives to their particular causes. Our nation is a better place because of what these concerned women have been able to accomplish.

Chapter 3

THE AWAKENING OF CHRISTIAN WOMEN IN AMERICA

I know this is going to sound unusual, but I am truly indebted to Bella Abzug, Gloria Steinem, Betty Friedan, and other radical feminists for the existence of Concerned Women for America (CWA), a group I founded in 1979 to combat the goals of the feminist movement. The blatantly pro-lesbian tactics of radical feminists at the National Women's Convention (held from November 18 through 21 of 1977 in Houston, Texas to celebrate International Women's Year) opened my eyes and the eyes of other Christian women across the nation who were involved in it.

I was attending a Christian women's conference at the Anaheim Convention Center, where I had been asked to give a short talk on the power of prayer in women's lives, when a long-time friend rushed up to me with a worried look on her face.

Gladys Dickelman, a delegate from Illinois to the National Women's Convention, had gone to the meeting as a passive observer. But she had quickly become an aggressive Christian activist, supporting a pro-family, pro-American position. Why the change? Not long after she arrived, the radicals began circulating an "enemy list," which targeted her and other Christian women as enemies of the goals of the convention. At the top of the list were these words: NOTICE: AVOID THESE WOMEN. DO NOT VOTE FOR THEM. THEY ARE PAID BY SECRET ORGANIZATIONS. THEY ARE TRYING TO TAKE AWAY FROM US OUR HARD WON RIGHTS. THEY ARE ENEMIES OF THE STATE. DO NOT BELIEVE THEM REGARDLESS OF WHAT THEY SAY.

Gladys and her friends were visibly shaken. They knew this was no ordinary convention. It was not in any way an open forum for the honest exchange of ideas on women's issues. The feminists were firmly in control from the beginning to the end.

The convention hall was filled with booths sponsored by various revolutionary groups: an organization of prostitutes known as COYOTE (Call Off Your Old Tired Ethics), Worker's World Party, Youth Against War and Fascism, Radical Women, the Freedom Socializing Committee, Institute for Policy Studies, the National Gay Task Force, and many others.

Many of the booths featured a variety of lesbian products from jewelry to T-shirts with statements like "Warm Fuzzy Dyke" (a slang word for lesbian) on them. One booth was selling electric vibrators and dildoes.

On sale were lesbian pamphlets with titles such as "What Lesbians Do," "Good Vibrations," "Self Sexuality for Women," "The Love My Body Book," and others. One such booklet, entitled "A Lesbian Guide," proudly stated on its cover: "This booklet was prepared by the National Gay Task Force and officially approved by the National Commission on the Observance of International Women's Year." In addition, pro-lesbian and anti-male buttons were everywhere: "Mother nature is a

Lesbian." "A Woman without a Man is like a Fish without a Bicycle." "Trust in God, She will provide." One of the most shocking buttons read, "Don't litter—use birth control."

At one point the delegates were treated to the spectacle of a motorcycle gang of denim-clad lesbians roaring around the convention center. Many of these women wore tight T-shirts bearing the words: "What are you staring at, PIG?" Chants of "Three, five, seven, nine, lesbians are riding high" filled the auditorium. Later, hundreds of lesbians began stomping their feet and screaming, "Dyke, Dyke, Dyke!"

The political and social agenda of the Houston convention was even more disturbing. Ignoring fairness or parliamentary procedures, the feminists pushed through such resolutions as the ratification of the Equal Rights Amendment; the "right" of homosexuals and lesbians to teach in public schools and to have custody of children; federally funded abortion on demand; approval of abortion for teen-agers without parental knowledge or consent; federal government involvement in twenty-four-hour-a-day child care centers and more.

Only about 20 percent of the two thousand delegates were conservative or Christian women. They were unable to exercise any influence, but under the leadership of Rosemary Thomson and Dianne Edmondson, they did draft a Minority Report. Unfortunately, the leadership of the International Women's Year refused to accept the Minority Report.

As it turned out, twelve organizations maintained a tight control of the convention. They were: National Organization for Women, American Civil Liberties Union, League of Women Voters, the Women's Political Caucus, ERAmerica, National Federation of Business and Professional Women's Clubs, the Citizens Library Council on the Status of Women, the National Gay Task Force, Church Women United, American Association of University Women, the Women's Alliance Coalition of Labor Women, and Common Cause.

Not only had the feminists manipulated the outcome of the National Convention, but they had also been successful in controlling the state conventions.

Another friend of mine, Mary Schmitz, had been an eyewitness to the California International Women's Year Convention. As she observed shortly after the convention, "The California meeting was completely controlled, manipulated, and used exclusively by a small segment of women representing the radical women's lib and lesbian points of view only."[1]

Again, the convention was filled with booths featuring such items as vibrators and lesbian coloring books, which contained detailed drawings of female genitalia and other pornography. One group had prepared a display to demonstrate how women could perform self-abortions.

I learned later that the Hawaii International Women's Year Convention had featured lesbian pantomimes on such things as how lesbian women could have sex in pay toilets.

It is difficult for me to convey the feelings I experienced after listening to Gladys Dickelman unfold the story of the Houston convention. I was nauseous and filled with despair as I realized that those feminists were claiming to speak for all women in America. In my heart I knew that was a lie. Those feminists had managed to convince Congress to spend five million dollars of our tax money to hold state conventions and then this grand finale at Houston, which seemed to be a Marxist/lesbian circus, manipulated and controlled from the beginning by a dissident group of feminists who were demanding federal intervention into our lives.

My nausea soon changed to rage, and I determined in my heart that I would do whatever was necessary to raise up a standard of righteousness against feminism.

On the return drive to San Diego from the Anaheim convention, five friends and I talked nonstop about the Houston convention and the feminist movement. We had been trying to live as good Christian women, being decent mothers and citizens, but we had been completely ignorant of the social forces that threatened to destroy our families and our nation. It was time to get busy and do something to oppose the feminist movement—or any movement that purposed to destroy the sanctity of our homes.

Not long after that, nine of us met at a friend's home to discuss what we could do to alert the Christian community to the feminist and humanist threat. We talked and prayed together many times during the next few weeks as the Lord gradually gave us a vision for what He wanted us to do. During the next four months we held something like sixty "coffees" with other women in the San Diego area. We met to discuss the Equal Rights Amendment and other associated issues. Our objective was to get support for a massive rally in San Diego.

My friend Mary Schmitz spoke on the Equal Rights Amendment as the keynote speaker at that rally. My husband, Tim, also delivered a powerful speech on the homosexual movement in America. More than twelve hundred people attended our first meeting—and from that moment forward, our lives have never been the same.

We realized that anything we tried to accomplish had

to be of the Lord or our work would be in vain. From its inception, CWA's activities have been based on prayer. Our motto reflects that premise: "Protecting the rights of the family through prayer and action."

In the early days of CWA, we held "coffees" in various homes around the San Diego area. We gathered research materials on the feminist movement and other issues of importance to the family, and we distributed them to people who were interested in our work. As we received more and more requests from outside of California, we took steps to incorporate and establish ourselves as a bona fide legal organization.

After CWA's incorporation in January 1979, its future began to take shape right before our eyes. It was a sovereign work of the Lord, to be sure. I can remember how thrilled we all were in March 1979 to find that we had 24 members. By May we had 88. And by June it had grown to 229.

In the spring of 1979, we managed to put together our first monthly CWA newsletter with a headline that read, "New Organization Formed." We described the purpose of CWA to our new audience. That first newsletter featured a listing of pending legislation, a discussion of the International Year of the Child, a speaker's calendar, a feature on the so-called "Children's Rights Movement," and suggestions for action.

We spent nearly a year gathering materials on the International Year of the Child (IYC) and exposing its pro-statist, anti-family bias. The IYC was our first educational battle. It is so important that I will discuss it in the next chapter. In November 1979, just ten months after we'd been incorporated, we had received requests for membership from twenty-seven states. Within a year after we were formed, we had 655 members and more than 20,000 women who had committed themselves to supporting our pro-family objectives.

We were filling a void that had existed far too long. Traditional Christian women desperately needed to have a voice in the affairs of this nation. The radical feminists, by default, were managing to press their antifamily, anti-God objectives in state legislatures and in the federal government as well.

We were determined to stand in opposition to them. But we knew we had to do more than simply oppose feminism; we knew we must actively promote pro-family values in America. We quickly realized to stand merely *against* issues was inadequate; progress and lasting results would come from *forward* movements, and we set out to promote change.

No longer do the feminists have a monopoly. No longer can they claim to speak for *all* American women. We are here, hundreds of thousands now, telling the world that feminism is a false view of the world.

Chapter 4

EXPOSING THE CHILDREN'S RIGHTS MOVEMENT

Our exposure to the International Women's Year (IWY) fiasco in Houston showed me that we could expect far more feminist agitation for social change in America. IWY was only the beginning. The goals had been set for revolutionary social upheavals in our culture. It soon became obvious to me that the International Year of the Child (IYC) was simply a continuation of this feminist/socialist revolution. It was our task at CWA to investigate the background and purposes of IYC—and then to expose them and actively lobby against it.

To this end, we gathered materials from magazines, books, and pro-UN publications, consulted with leaders of other pro-family groups, and prepared an in-depth analysis of IYC for our members and supporters.

Our report began with these words of warning:

IYC stands for the International Year of the Child. We are told it was designed to put a fresh focus on children's concerns around the world, and it is represented by many to be an aid in helping the millions who suffer from some form of malnutrition and abuse. At a quick glance, this looks commendable, but today with all the subtle approaches of humanism, it is necessary to look beyond the surface. You owe it to yourself, and most of all, *your* family, to examine the following: Who is behind the program? What is their philosophy? What are their goals? What agencies are backing IYC? How is it already affecting my family?

It was feminist leader Betty Friedan, author of *The Feminine Mystique*, founder of the National Organization for Women (*NOW*), and signer of the Humanist Manifesto II, who revealed the Marxist roots of the International Year of the Child. In an account of her participation in the World Conference for Women in Mexico City, she observed, "I had a curious luncheon invitation from a woman involved with the old-time Communist Women's group, the International Federation of Democratic Women [WIDF]....They said, did I know, by the way, it was they who introduced the resolution to make 1975 International Women's Year?...I hadn't known that."[1]

Interestingly enough, *U.S. News & World Report*, (August 7, 1978), featured a two-page article entitled "Russia's Massive Campaign to Blacken U.S. Image" (pp.42-44), discussing Moscow's numerous communist front groups and their interlocking subversion around the world. The Women's International Democratic Federation (WIDF), headquartered in East Berlin, was prominently displayed.

The WIDF enthusiastically supported the IYC and the International Women's Year in its publication, *Women of the Whole World*:

The WIDF is one of the non-governmental organizations that took action together with others in favour of the proclamation of the International Year of the Child. To-

34

day, our Declaration on the International Year of the Child, while pointing out that the rights of the child are closely linked with the problems of women and the whole of society, also states that *society as a whole is responsible for the fate of the child* [emphasis ours].[2]

To promote the state control of children, this Communist women's organization was the sponsor of the first International Year of the Child conference in October of 1977 in Prague, Czechoslovakia.

Through the influence of Marxists within the UN, our own government was used for Marxist purposes. Although 1979 was officially designated by President Jimmy Carter as the International Year of the Child, the objectives of IYC are still being carried on through a variety of nongovernmental organizations (NGOs). If you understand the real objectives of IYC and know what nongovernmental organizations are promoting IYC goals, you will easily recognize IYC propaganda when you come across it.

Our research revealed that the International Year of the Child was specifically designed to carry out the objectives of the Declaration of the Rights of the Child first proposed by the United Nations in 1959.

In this seemingly harmless declaration, the United Nations has mapped out a strategy for "nationalizing" all children of the world. A careful reading of this document leads me to believe that the UN does not support the basic unit of society, the family. The UN believes that it is the *government's* responsibility to take care of children, from the cradle to the grave. The UN and its supporters believe that parents are not usually competent to take proper care of their offspring.

In Principle 10 of this declaration, we read,

The child shall be protected from practices which may foster racial, religious and any other form of discrimination. He shall be brought up in a spirit of understanding, tolerance, friendship among peoples, peace and universal brotherhood, and in full consciousness that his energy and talents should be devoted to the service of his fellow men.

That sounds very noble until it is closely examined. The UN is saying that it is up to the government to determine what practices may foster racial, religious, or other forms of discrimination. Does being an anticommunist Christian promote a form of religious discrimination against Marxists? Using UN logic, this would certainly be the case.

Is a parent sowing seeds of hatred and discord in his children by teaching them to love their own country? According to a UNESCO booklet, *Toward World Understanding*, nationalism is a threat to world peace:

As long as the child breathes the poisoned air of nationalism, education in world-mindedness can produce only rather precarious results. As we have pointed out, it is frequently the family that infects the child with extreme nationalism. The school should therefore use the means described earlier to combat family attitudes that favor jingoism.[3]

The International Year of the Child seeks to "liberate" children from the poisoned atmosphere of nationalism, training all the children of the world to favor international socialism. In fact, one of the officially stated purposes of IYC is to "promote a new International Social and Economic Order as planned by the UN Social and Economic Council."[4]

The Declaration of the Rights of the Child also expresses concern over the health of all children. This, too, sounds laudible until scrutinized. The IYC Commission stated,

> While there are many definitions of health, the Commission chose the (UN) World Health Organization definition: "Health is a state of complete physical, mental and social well-being and not merely the absence of disease or infirmity." A child's health is influenced by many factors, such as food, the care and concern provided by parents and guardians, exercise, living conditions, family income, customs, habit and beliefs....How can we best prevent physical, sexual and emotional abuse of children?[5]

In other words, every aspect of a child's life should be under the watchful eye of government. A parent's beliefs, income, and habits are to be judged through the government's eyes. If a parent falls short of these guidelines, the child will be removed from the home.

If we, as Christians, were to fall under the authority of the United Nations' Declaration, all of us would probably lose our children—simply because of our Christian beliefs. Let me quote noted humanist sexologist Dr. Albert Ellis on the subject of religion:

> Religion is...directly opposed to the goals of mental health....It encourages a fanatic, obsessive-compulsive kind of commitment that is, in its own right, a form of mental illness....This close connection between mental illness and religion is inevitable and invariant....In the final analysis, then, religion is neurosis.[6]

Senator Orrin Hatch (R., Utah) was correct when he

made the following statement in the *Congressional Record*, March 26, 1979:

> The IYC may be a dangerous tool being used on people who are generally ignorant of its profound significance for the family unit. With its seemingly harmless name, the IYC appears to be a platform for pushing such liberal causes as abortion, federalized day care centers, expansion of the welfare state, and so forth, all of which increase the involvement of the Federal Government in the raising of children and the shaping of their value systems.[7]

What is even more ominous than the establishment of total government control over our children is the concept of the "wanted" child, advocated by UN spokesmen.

Professor Luke T. Lee, of the International Advisory Committee on Population and Law to the UNICEF Executive Board, once made this following statement:

> Forgotten are the rights of the child—to be born wanted in the sense that the parents indeed want the child to be born, and not just by accident; wanted in the sense that the society wants the child to be born as evidenced by the availability of adequate health care, food, housing, education, and job opportunities which society can provide to each and every child; and above all, wantedness in the sense that the child, if it had the choice, would have wanted to be born, especially if neither the parents nor the society really wants it.[8]

What he appears to be saying is that every child should be planned for and wanted by its parents and society. It seems to me the opposite is implied. If a child is not wanted by either the parent or society, what is to be done with it? It is to be murdered by abortion. If the child has the misfortune of being born with a handicap, it is to be starved to death by hospital personnel.

It is this kind of twisted logic that energizes and motivates the socialists/humanists within the United Nations.

The International Year of the Child was supported by such organizations as the American Civil Liberties Union, American Humanist Association, the National Organization for Women, American Association of University Women, NAACP, League of Women Voters, Amnesty International, CORE (Congress of Racial Equality), Planned Parenthood, and the Gray Panthers. These nongovernmental organizations are still actively promoting the objectives of IYC. (It is certainly no coincidence that many of these organizations were aggressively behind the International Women's Year and were also involved in the White House Conference on Families, which I will discuss in the next chapter.)

Much of what is known as the Child Advocacy Movement has sprung from the International Year of the Child. Self-proclaimed child advocates are usually nothing more than advocates of federal meddling in the private affairs of American families. Notice the increasing involvement of the federal government in such things as wife beating. There is absolutely no reason why the federal government has to become involved in an area that can easily be handled by local law enforcement officials.

Yet in the International Women's Year, the International Year of the Child, and the White House Conference on Families, the leadership has consistently pushed for greater government control over our lives. The pattern is consistent because those involved in these movements favor centralized governmental control and the abolition of the traditional family.

Concerned Women for America has consistently opposed any movement that seeks to usurp the responsibility of parents to bring up their children in the way they see fit. We oppose any group that would seek to control the value system of our youth or substitute governmental care for parental love and guidance.

We need only look at Sweden to see what can happen to a society that adopts the principles of the IYC. As of July 1, 1979, it became illegal in Sweden for parents to punish their children physically. No spanking, slapping, or physical contact is allowed. The new law restricts much more than physical punishment; it prohibits "any act which, for the purpose of punishing, causes the child physical injury or pain, even if the disturbance is mild and passing" and any action that treats the child in a "humiliating manner." The definition of what is humiliating is left up to the court system to decide. Forcing a child to attend Sunday school could conceivably be humiliating to the child and result in a criminal penalty.

I can remember when I was in Sweden several years ago and had the opportunity of talking to a very sad twenty-one-year-old woman. She said that when she was twelve, she had been spanked severely by her father—a spanking she admits she deserved. But instead of accepting her punishment, she reported him to the authorities, accusing him of treating her cruelly. She was quickly removed from the family and was forced to spend the next six years in a child care center. She lamented that since then she had been involved in "every sin of young people."

The Word of God *commands* us, as parents, to discipline and train our children. Ephesians 6:4 tells us: "Fathers, do not exasperate your children; instead, bring them up in the training and instruction of the Lord." *Not* to discipline our children properly is to violate the clear commands of our God. How do Christians in Sweden handle this dilemma? I honestly don't know. But I do know that we must never allow what happened in Sweden to happen in America.

Did we, as an organization of Christian women, have any impact on the International Year of the Child? We certainly did not change the preconceived notions of those who promoted the internationalization of our children. But we did manage to awaken a good number of Americans to the reality of what the United Nations and the humanists were (and are) trying to do to destroy the traditional family unit.

The radical organizations pushing for the internationalization of our children were soon to move on to another project—the White House Conference on Families. As we'll see in the next chapter, this conference was simply a continuation of their efforts to impose government control over the rights of the family. Those organizations were going to be surprised at the opposition they encountered from CWA and other pro-family coalitions. The Christians were finally awakening—and acting!

Chapter 5

THE WHITE HOUSE ATTACK ON FAMILIES

With the major educational battles against the International Women's Year and the International Year of the Child barely behind us, we began collecting materials on the upcoming White House Conference on Families (WHCF) in 1980, which came about as the result of a campaign promise by President Jimmy Carter.

It didn't take too much work to discover that the White House Conference on Families was going to be another installment in the never-ending attack on the family by the feminist/socialist/humanist coalition in America. Fortunately, we had gained some political savvy and wisdom in our battles against IWY and IYC. We began our educational campaign by first detailing the origins of this White House conference and then providing information to our members on how they could become delegates in their states to the national meetings, which were scheduled to be held in Baltimore (June 5-7), Minneapolis (June 19-21), and Los Angeles (July 10-12).

According to an official brochure, the ostensible purpose of this conference was

> to identify ways to strengthen and support American families. It is an attempt to involve families themselves,

as well as scholars, professionals, and policy makers in a long overdue assessment of how government and our major private institutions help, hurt, or neglect families.[1]

We knew otherwise, of course. The most obvious tip-off as to the feminist/humanist leanings of this conference came from examining the backgrounds of the forty-one members of the National Advisory Committee, a committee handpicked by President Jimmy Carter.

The "chairperson" of this committee was former Congressman Jim Guy Tucker of Arkansas; Deputy "chairpersons" were liberal New York Lt. Governor Mario M. Cuomo; Coretta Scott King; Patsy Mink, then head of Americans for Democratic Action, a liberal activist group; Eleanor C. Smeal, then president of NOW; Maryann Mahaffey, a former president of the National Association of Social Workers; and Jesse Jackson, head of Operation Push (and a good friend of PLO terrorist leader Yasir Arafat) and a candidate for the presidency of the United States in 1984.[2]

As far as we could tell, only one woman, Barbara B. Smith, a Mormon who was head of the Church Relief Society held to a consistent pro-family position. One out of forty-one!

Serving as an unofficial but highly influential coalition of liberal groups manipulating conference objectives were such organizations as Planned Parenthood; National Gay Task Force; American Association of Sex Educators, Counselors & Therapists; National Council of Churches; Zero Population Growth; and National Alliance of Optional Parenthood.[3] I was absolutely amazed to learn that the National Gay Task Force was actually one of the groups appointed to the National Advisory Council of the White House conference! What could be more ridiculous than having lesbians and homosexual men determining what is good for families?

Yet as we were soon to learn, the White House Conference on Families (WHCF) was not dealing with what you and I normally consider a family: a husband and wife caring for children. One of the biggest controversies to come out of this conference was an argument over the definition of what a family is. No one could agree.

The lesbians, homosexual men, and feminists accepted the following definition provided by the Department of Health, Education, and Welfare:

> Whether by blood, religious or legal contract, or simply by mutual consent, any individuals sharing or choosing to share each other's lives and/or living space for any emotional, economic, or social reasons may be functioning as a family....Makers of public policy should, in general, respect those persons' views of their own supportive arrangements.[4]

That definition was rejected by Christians because it distorted the traditional meaning of family to include *any* kind of living arrangement, from "married" lesbians raising children to weird hippie communes.

By redefining the meaning of the word *family*, the feminists and homosexual men hope to gain the legal right to live their perverted lifestyle protected by the laws of the land.

Eleanor Smeal, then president of the National Organization for Women, made this statement at WHCF hearings in Washington, D.C.:

> Lesbians and gay men and their families have a right to an end to custody judgments that deny gay parents and their children continuation of a loving parent-child rela-

tionship; enactment of civil rights laws at the local, state and federal levels which would provide lesbians and gay men the same protections now provided to others....[5]

Rosemary Thomson, a delegate to the National Women's Convention and author of *The Price of LIBerty*, clearly stated the true objectives of the White House conference in an interview in *Human Events*, a conservative, weekly Washington newspaper. "In a nutshell," said Rosemary,

the White House Conference is IWY [International Women's Year] revisited. At IWY, they called in the name of women's rights for ERA, abortion, gay rights, federal day-care, minimum guaranteed annual wage, national health insurance, to name a few. Now comes the White House Conference on Families, and at the regional hearings all around the country, in the name of strengthening the family, we need ERA, national health insurance, the whole ball of wax. So it appears that the White House Conference is intending to implement the resolutions that came out of IWY.[6]

As soon as I had learned about the White House conference, I was in contact with pro-family groups all over the nation. We were determined to make our voices heard in those meetings. To that end, we joined in a National Pro-Family Coalition on the White House Conference on Families. Tim and I were named co-chairmen of this coalition and were honored to work with more than 150 other pro-family, pro-life, pro-American organizations in developing strategies to make our views known in the White House conference meetings.

In our Statement of Principles, drafted by Dr. Onalee

McGraw of the Heritage Foundation, we declared the following:

> The most important function performed by the family is rearing and character forming of children....God has given to parents [this] right and responsibility....We are unalterably opposed to government policies and judicial decisions which permit or promote government-funded "services" of counseling, contraception and abortion to minor children without parental knowledge and consent....We believe that the right of parents to rear their children according to their religious beliefs is a fundamental order of God and nature. It must not be undermined or counteracted by any government action.[7]

Our pro-family coalition also developed a five-point moral platform:

1. Definition of the Family: A family consists of persons who are related by blood, adoption, or by a legal marriage between unrelated individuals of the opposite sex and children of this relationship.

2. Abortion: Any enumeration of human rights must begin with the right to life from the moment of conception.

3. ERA: We support the historic American principle that laws relating to marriage and domestic relations are exclusively in the jurisdiction of the states, not the federal government. We oppose the ratification of any Equal Rights Amendment which would grant the Congress authority to legislate in the area of family law, as in the presently pending so-called Equal Rights Amendment.

4. Family Protection Act: We recognize that solutions to family problems will not be found in a proliferation of government programs. Therefore we endorse Senator

Paul Laxalt's Family Protection Act (S.1808 as amended), and the family-protecting approaches embodied in it, which encourage family, community, and local initiatives to help families solve their problems.

5. Family Rights: Parents have the God-given right and responsibility to raise their children in accordance with His laws, and children have the right to learn moral values in the family without external interference. Thus, no program of manipulation in matters of education, family life, moral behavior, contraception, or abortion services shall be permitted without prior parental knowledge and consent.

Our educational campaign began to pay off quickly. In the middle of 1979, Virginia became the first state to hold its statewide conference on families as a prelude to the national conferences. Thanks to our educational efforts—and the diligent work of hundreds of conservative and/or Christian women in Virginia, the pro-family coalition was able to garner twenty-two out of twenty-four delegates to the national election.

The feminists were alarmed and outraged that traditional women had upset their carefully prepared plans to monopolize all state meetings. The National Advisory Committee counterattacked by refusing to keep the pro-family coalition informed on the activities of the various state meetings.

They also began changing the rules for the selection of delegates to the conference. It became obvious to the feminists that free elections might result in Christian victories in the state meetings. So in January, the rules were changed; delegates would no longer be elected but would instead be selected by state coordinators. Thus, in many states the public was not allowed to participate—

and Christians were denied the opportunity to voice their views.

As a result of feminist manipulation, the first White House Conference on Families, held in Baltimore, came out with a totally feminist agenda. Resolutions were passed advocating the right to abortion, the Equal Rights Amendment, nondiscrimination against homosexuals, national health insurance, and a guaranteed annual income for poor families (thirteen thousand dollars for a family of four).

A group of pro-family delegates staged a mass walkout at the Baltimore conference to protest the manipulation of the meeting by the humanists and feminists.

In the Minneapolis meeting, the pro-family forces were strong enough to get several resolutions passed including a denunciation of secular humanism and a definition of family that excluded homosexual liaisons. A resolution favoring the ERA was passed, however, and support for the human life amendment was defeated.

Realizing that the pro-family viewpoint would be censored or ignored, we decided to organize our own conference on the family on the West Coast.

Billed as an "Alternate White House Conference," we held an "American Pro-Family Conference" at the Long Beach Civic Auditorium on July 12, 1980—the same day the final WHCF was being held in Los Angeles.

Our pro-family conference was sponsored by such groups as American Life Lobby, Christian Family Renewal, Christian Voice, The Conservative Caucus, Concerned Women for America, Family Life Seminars, Eagle Forum, Gospel Light Publications, Heritage Foundation, Intercessors for America, The Right Woman, Moral Majority, and others.

More than seven thousand enthusiastic delegates from eleven states came to our conference to hear such dynamic speakers as pro-life leader Dr. Mildred Jefferson; Dr. Jerry Falwell; Dr. Bill Bright, head of Campus Crusade for Christ; Mrs. Phyllis Schlafly, founder of STOP ERA; Howard Phillips of Conservative Caucus; Charles Keating of Citizens for Decency through Law; Cleon Skousen of the Freemen Institute; Senator Jesse Helms; and my husband, Tim. They delivered powerful speeches on such issues as pornography, the importance of the family, and the threat of humanism and homosexuality to the stability of our society.

The conference passed resolutions opposing abortion, the Equal Rights Amendment, and laws favoring homosexual lifestyles. We voted to support a voluntary prayer amendment and local community standards to wipe out pornography. We also passed a resolution calling for a Senate investigation of the procedures used in choosing delegates to the national White House Conference on Families.

All our resolutions and concerns were delivered directly to President Jimmy Carter, bypassing the WHCF. He did nothing about them, of course, but at least we had made a public statement showing our opposition to the feminist agenda proposed by the tightly controlled White House Conference on Families.

The final report of the WHCF did not deal with the issues of homosexuality or abortion, but concentrated instead on alcohol and drug abuse, tax and housing changes, media violence, discrimination, energy, and inflation policies.

The report turned out to be less revolutionary than the radicals had hoped for. Our pro-family coalition can take much of the credit for toning down their radicalism. We also demonstrated to the liberals and radicals that we were alive, well, and gaining strength. We were going to be monitoring them and exposing their activities through a rapidly growing network of pro-family groups.

The opposition we had faced from the feminists was actually beneficial to our pro-family movement. We began to discover that we could ally ourselves with men and women of all faiths, joining together to work in unity against a common enemy.

Christians were even beginning to work together in temporary coalitions with cult groups who shared the same concerns for religious freedom. We were not compromising our strongly held religious beliefs, but we were slowly and surely learning that we could agree to battle a common enemy even if our own theological differences could never be resolved with these non-Christian groups. (The Left had learned long ago to work with various groups to achieve a common objective.)

I knew that once we could lay aside our theological differences—once we could agree to disagree on theology and then work side-by-side for a common goal—we could finally become a truly effective force for righteousness in this nation. I should probably point out that our main emphasis has been on developing working relationships with women in all Christian denominations; our alliances with cults has been (and probably will continue to be) infrequent.

Our pro-family conference was thrilling to me not only because we made a public statement opposing the WHCF but also because I could see a powerful pro-family coalition being formed, which will eventually win against the feminists and humanists. I am totally convinced of that.

Chapter 6

THE STRUGGLE AGAINST A UNISEX SOCIETY

As you have probably realized, Concerned Women for America is an activist women's organization. We are not simply an educational organization publishing pro-family materials. We feel the need for, and importance of, being in the forefront of a great spiritual revival in this country. Prayer *and* action are essential if we are to protect our families and our personal freedoms.

One of the most exciting and rewarding educational battles I was engaged in during the early years of CWA was the fight against the passage of the Equal Rights Amendment.

I am not against equal rights for women. I am totally in favor of equal pay for equal work; I support a woman's right to be free from sexual harassment on the job. What I am against, however, is an amendment to the constitution that is a cleverly disguised tool to invite total government control over our lives. As you'll soon see, there are already enough laws on the books to protect the rights of women in the marketplace.

The Equal Rights Amendment is a deceptively simple document, which has three short sections. Let me quote the ERA and then explain what these fifty-two words really mean to all women.

SECTION ONE: Equality of rights under the law shall not be denied or abridged by the United States or by any state on account of sex. SECTION TWO: The Congress shall have the power to enforce, by appropriate legislation, the provisions of this article. SECTION THREE: This amendment shall take effect two years after the date of ratification.

That's all it says. It looks simple, just, and fair. Unfortunately, this facade of simplicity and justice could demolish nearly every social and legal tradition in America. The ERA, if passed, would literally transform every women's issue into a complex constitutional question to be decided by our liberal court system.

This is not just my opinion, it is the opinion of constitutional scholars—on both sides of the issue. In the *Congressional Record*, March 22, 1972, Senator Sam J. Ervin analyzed the devastating consequences that would result if the Equal Rights Amendment were ever passed:

> If the Equal Rights for Women Amendment is approved, I believe that the Supreme Court will reach the conclusion that the ERA annuls every existing Federal and state law making any distinction between men and women however reasonable such distinction might be in particular cases, and forever robs the Congress and the legislatures of the fifty states of the Constitutional power to enact any such laws at any time in the future. I am not alone in entertaining this fear.

When the so-called Equal Rights Amendment was under consideration in 1953, Roscoe Pound of the Harvard Law School and other outstanding scholars joined one of America's greatest legal scholars, Paul A. Freund of the Harvard Law School, in a statement opposing the Equal Rights Amendment. . . . This statement made these indisputable observations:

> If anything about this proposed amendment is clear, it is that it would transform every provision of law concerning women into a constitutional issue to be ultimately resolved by the Supreme Court of the United States. Every statutory and common law provision dealing with the manifold relations of women in society would be forced to run the gauntlet of attack on constitutional grounds.[1]

Under the ERA, we would be victimized by federal judges who would, most likely, view the amendment in absolute terms. No exceptions would be allowed for any sex-based laws. There are numerous federal and state laws that make a distinction between males and females—and legitimately so. It is not discriminatory, for instance, to prohibit a woman from working as a shoeshine attendant in a men's public restroom. Yet if the ERA were passed, there could be no such law because it is based upon sex.

The Equal Rights Amendment would mandate that women and men be treated in the same manner—regardless of how much violence it might do to personal privacy or the safety of women. This is especially true when it comes to military combat situations.

Let me list a few of the terrible consequences that would result if the ERA should ever become part of our Constitution:

1. There would be complete integration of the sexes. Men and women would lose their right to privacy. Professor Paul Freund, of the Harvard Law School has testified that the ERA would require that "there be no

segregation of the sexes in prisons, reform schools, public restrooms, and other public facilities." This would include all public and private schools (including religious), college dormitories, and hospital rooms (*Congressional Record*, March 22, 1972, p. S4543).

I know it sounds somewhat absurd to speak of unisex restrooms, but there is no prohibition under the ERA to prevent a federal judge from interpreting it to mean that absolutely no facilities can be segregated on account of sex. If the ERA is to apply to sexual discrimination in the same manner as civil rights laws deal with race, it is likely that unisex restrooms would be mandated. Separate but equal bathrooms for blacks and whites are outlawed. The ERA would undoubtedly banish separate but equal bathrooms for the sexes.

The ERA would certainly require integrated prison facilities. According to a Virginia Attorney General's report on the ERA, "Separate colleges, hospitals, and prisons would have to be sexually integrated. Not only must separate colleges and prisons be abolished, but facilities within those institutions, such as dormitories, would have to be sex neutral."[2]

2. Homosexuality would be legalized. In an article entitled "The Legality of Homosexual Marriage," published in the *Yale Law Journal*, the authors conclude, "A statute or administrative policy which permits a man to marry a woman, subject to certain regulatory restrictions, but categorically denies him the right to marry another man, clearly entails a classification along sexual lines."[3] The ERA would clearly legalize homosexual "marriages." If no discrimination is allowed against anyone for his or her sexual activities, then homosexuals would be given legal protection under the Constitution. They would be given the right to marry, adopt children,

openly teach our children, and spread their sexual perversions with impunity.

3. Women would be required to register for the draft and engage in combat alongside men. The *Yale Law Journal*, April 1971, contains an excellent article on the ERA, written by pro-ERA professor Thomas I. Emerson. He points out that not only will women be in combat units, but also they will have no right to privacy or special treatment. In addition, mothers will be just as likely to be sent to war as fathers.

Deferment policy, Emerson says, "could provide that one, but not both, of the parents would be deferred. For example, whichever parent was called first might be eligible for service; the remaining parent, male or female, would be deferred."[4] A mother could be drafted, and the father, therefore, would be exempted from military service.

4. Sodomy or adultery laws would be abolished. Thomas Emerson's article goes on to point out that "courts will most likely invalidate sodomy or adultery laws that contain discriminatory provisions, instead of solving the constitutional problems by extending them to cover men and women alike." In addition, "seduction laws, statutory rape laws, laws prohibiting obscene language in the presence of women, prostitution and 'manifest danger laws'...Equal Rights Amendment would not permit such laws, which base their sex discriminatory classification on social stereotypes."

5. Laws that now require the husband to provide for his wife and children would have to be abolished because they "discriminate" in the favor of women. Women would be legally responsible for 50 percent of the support of the family.

In Pennsylvania, which has a state ERA, the court

ruled that a husband did not have to pay for his wife's "necessaries," noting that these include not only medical care, but also food, clothing, and shelter (in *Albert Einstein Medical Center v. Nathans*). The court further stated that the common law concept obligating the husband to pay for his wife's necessaries is "repugnant to the Equal Rights Amendment."[5]

In another case, the Pennsylvania court ruled that the law requiring a father to support his minor child was invalid (*Conway v. Dana*). The court stated that this "presumption is clearly a vestige of the past and incompatible with the present recognition of equality of the sexes."[6]

6. Wives will lose their right to draw social security based on their husbands' earnings. Instead, "the homemaker would contribute social security taxes just like any other self-employed person now covered," Sylvia Porter wrote in her financial column. "Of course, those taxes would have to come out of the earnings of the husband, and it might be charged that he would be paying taxes twice...once on his own earnings and once on the assumed earnings of his wife as a homemaker. But, this would be fair and equitable, for if the husband had to hire someone to perform his wife's household duties...he would be required to pay social security on those earnings."[7]

7. Single sex schools would be abolished, as would groups such as the Boy Scouts, Girl Scouts, and private clubs that admit only one sex. This sounds farfetched, but it's true. One lawsuit against a single-sex organization would give a liberal judge the opportunity to strictly interpret the ERA and declare any organization that is limited to one sex unconstitutional. Do we really wish to give judges that kind of power?

8. Churches and church colleges and schools would be seriously jeopardized. It would be "unconstitutional" to refuse to admit homosexuals or women to the clergy.

9. Abortion would be a constitutional right. No discrimination based on sex would be allowed.

In his congressional statement, Sam Ervin quoted from Patrick M. Craney's book, *Equal Rights Amendment v. A Human Life Amendment*, and warned, "ERA will give every woman a Constitutional right to have an abortion at will. Since men cannot be compelled to have children, the only way (by law) to place women on an equal basis is to give them the right to abortion to keep from having children."[8]

These are just a few examples of the kind of social disruption we can expect if the ERA is ever passed. Our court system could be glutted with lawsuits filed by rabid feminists. The whole social fabric of our nation could be torn apart by such litigation.

The feminists continually cry about "equal pay for equal work" and demand "equal treatment" as well. Yet there are already sufficient laws on the books which guarantee women the same rights as men.

As I pointed out in my book, *I Am A Woman By God's Design*,

> Equal pay for equal work is covered by: Civil Rights Act of 1964; Equal Pay Act of 1963; Equal Employment Opportunity Act of 1972. Equal treatment is covered by: Fourteenth Amendment; Higher Education Act of 1972; Comprehensive Health Manpower Training Act of 1971; Nurse Training Act of 1971; Comprehensive Employment and Training Act of 1973; Federal Equal Credit Opportunity Act of 1975.[9]

I admit that not all women receive that same pay for

the same work as men. If a woman feels she is being discriminated against, she should take advantage of the protection provided under the laws mentioned above. If discrimination is occurring, it can be remedied by local, state, or regional equal employment opportunity commissions. We *do not need* an Equal Rights Amendment to protect our rights. We need to stand up for them ourselves.

If you would like a well documented discussion of the ERA and its ramifications, I would suggest you obtain a copy of *The Equal Rights Amendment—Myths and Realities*, written by Senator Orrin G. Hatch of Utah. Or for a shorter look at the ERA, you might wish to order CWA's ERA pamphlets—one a legal analysis of the ERA, written by our attorney Michael Farris, and the other an examination of the dangers of the state-passed ERAs. Both of these pamphlets will give you a better understanding of the dangers of the ERA to the stability of the family.

CWA Enters the ERA Battle in Illinois

Our opposition to the ERA took us to Illinois in 1980. We knew from our sources in Illinois that the feminists had targeted this key state for a massive propaganda attack to push for the ERA passage. Illinois was a symbol to the feminists, since it was the only northern industrial state that had not yet ratified the Equal Rights Amendment.

The National Organization for Women poured more than one million dollars into this battle. They were even shipping in NOW "missionaries"—women who had volunteered to leave their husbands and children to travel all over the country for six months to fight for passage of the ERA. In addition, President Jimmy Carter made telephone calls to Illinois legislators who were holding out against the ERA.

In light of these activities, we weren't really certain how successful we would be, even though the Illinois legislature had voted down the ERA ten times in the past. One thing about the feminists—they never give up. They keep pressing on until they win. That's why we need to have the same perseverance in opposing them.

We decided that the best way to fight passage was to inform the public and put pressure on the legislators. With that in mind, we contracted with a professional advertising agency in San Diego to help us develop some hard-hitting television spots on the ERA controversy. The four thirty-second spots, which used professional actors and actresses, cost more than thirty thousand dollars to develop, produce, and air. But it was well worth the effort. These spots were aired in the Springfield, Illinois, area a total of 246 times, just prior to the scheduled vote on ERA. In addition, we sent personal letters by registered mail to the state representatives and state senators to express our opposition to the ERA.

CWA also held a press conference with Illinois representatives Betty Hoxsey, Mary Lou Sumner, Penny Pullen, and Mary Lou Kent. During this conference we all shared our concerns for America's future.

Our media blitz paid off! The ERA was again defeated in Illinois—for the eleventh time! We had helped to assure its defeat. With only forty thousand dollars pitted against a NOW budget of one million dollars, we had knocked down Goliath. That victory against the feminist movement was particularly satisfying to me. I recall the night I was in the capitol building in Springfield, just prior to the important ERA vote. I was on the rotunda as an observer, watching hundreds of feminists crowded together, chanting ERA slogans. I felt as though an alien force had invaded the state capitol and was seeking to overthrow it.

A humanistic force is dividing this nation into warring political and social camps. We no longer think of ourselves as Americans but as conservatives, liberals, feminists. I believe many of our social problems have been fomented by conscious agents of communism. They have simply carried out communist doctrine: divide the nation into warring classes in an effort to weaken us, sap our strength, and destroy us.

I consider the feminist movement to be a serious threat to the stability of this nation. Let's see what they propose for future Americans.

"Feminism is the path to humanism, and it is humanism that is the goal," Gloria Steinam said at the Nevada State Women's Conference.

Since humanism is a word that has been bandied about so much it has almost lost its meaning, let's stop briefly to define it. The first definition in *The American Heritage Dictionary* is "a doctrine or attitude that is concerned primarily with human beings and their values, capacities, and achievements." Man is supreme here, not God.

The creed of the British Humanist Association states,

I believe in no god and no hereafter. It is immoral to indoctrinate children with such beliefs. Schools have no right to do so, nor indeed, have parents....I believe in a non-religious social morality....Unborn babies are not

people. I am as yet unsure whether the grossly handicapped are people in the real sense.

Karl Marx took the obvious next step in his definition: "Humanism is the denial of God and the total affir-
mation of man....Humanism is really nothing else but
Marxism."[10]

Gloria Steinem seems to have some of these same
goals for society. "By the year 2000 we will, I hope, raise
our children to believe in human potential, not God."[11]

Certainly some feminists are advocating socialism.
The Document: Declaration of Feminism says, "Women...understand the need for a socialist revolution.
Feminism rests on the belief that it is up to women to
...join hands to build a Feminist-Socialist Revolution."[12]

Other goals of feminism are just as apparent. In a
speech in Houston, Texas, Gloria Steinem said, "We
have to abolish and reform the institution of legal marriage."

Some feminists even deny women the right to choose
homemaking as a career. "No woman should be allowed
to stay at home to raise her children," Simone De-
Beauvoir said in *The Second Sex.* "Women should not
have that choice, precisely because if there is such a
choice, too many women will make that one."

Finally, radical feminists are advocating a new concept of sexuality—liberated sexuality, which "is freedom
from oppressive sexual stereotyping, freedom to choose
heterosexuality, homosexuality, bi-sexuality or a-sexual-
ity, but not to be bound by them," according to *The Document: Declaration of Feminism.*[13]

The New York chapter of NOW has even published a
pamphlet, "Struggle to End Sex Bias." Jean O'Leary, co-
executive director of the National Gay Task Force and an

avowed lesbian, gives these recommendations for ending sex bias in the schools:

1. School counselors be required to take courses in which a positive view of lesbianism is presented.
2. Students be encouraged to explore alternate lifestyles, including lesbianism.
3. Lesbian books be encouraged.
4. Lesbian clubs be set up.
5. Lesbian studies be instituted.[14]

Is this the society you and I choose to live in? Not I. And I wonder how many women who consider themselves to be feminist sympathizers really advocate this agenda.

To expose feminist philosophies for what they truly are, CWA is presenting a slide presentation, "The Facade of Feminism." If you have not already seen it, I would urge you to call CWA and schedule a showing in your community. Your eyes will be opened! In addition, we have made available a booklet called "Notes on the Facade of Feminism," which provides documented background material on this ideology. Other similar slide presentations are in various stages of production.

The thrilling victory against the ERA in Illinois propelled Concerned Women for America further ahead as an effective Christian women's organization. Shortly after this victory, I proudly informed our CWA board of directors that we'd grown to more than one hundred thousand members. It was evident that the "silent majority" among Christian women was awakening to the realities of the world around them. They were being shaken out of their lethargy, ignorance, and "churchianity."

Putting Our Representatives on the Record

Not too long after our stunning victory in Illinois, our staff developed a questionnaire which was sent to every political candidate running for office in a state that had not yet approved the Equal Rights Amendment. We were determined to force these potential legislators into making their moral and political views known to our membership. To ensure that each candidate received this questionnaire, we sent it by certified mail, return receipt requested. That way we would have a record of those who responded and those who chose to ignore our questions.

In the certified letter, I told each candidate, "I am writing to ask for your *careful consideration* of issues of major importance facing our nation. I have enclosed a questionnaire for you, the results of which will be distributed to our membership of over 120,000, other related organizations, and the news media."

In order to get an accurate picture of each candidate's political stand, we asked such questions as, "Do you favor more government programs to assist families (i.e., domestic violence appropriations, government-funded child care centers)? Do you believe that a woman has the right to terminate her pregnancy for any reason? Do you favor the amendment to the Constitution known as the Equal Rights Amendment (ERA)? In cases of child abuse or domestic violence, do you favor federal government involvement? Do you believe local communities should have the right to establish obscenity standards without First Amendment interference by federal courts?"

We were generally pleased with the results of this survey. I believe we got some genuinely honest answers. It wasn't long before we published them for our membership and for the press. We think it is essential that every registered voter knows exactly where the candidates stand on the moral issues facing this nation. CWA has continued to report the voting record of all elected federal candidates for the benefit of our members and friends. We had long ago lost any illusions about the kind of struggle in which we were engaged. We realized that the feminist movement was deadly serious about converting our nation into a unisex, socialist society.

As we continued to do battle against the Equal Rights Amendment, other skirmishes began to heat up in other sections of the country. We could sense that we were being prepared for costly legal confrontations with the secular humanists.

Chapter 7

PRAYER—THE QUIET STRENGTH OF CWA

Long before Concerned Women for America became a powerful, nationwide women's organization, I knew that it had to be founded on a solid basis. One Scripture passage that kept running through my mind over and over again was from Ephesians 5:13-17, where Paul, inspired by the Holy Spirit, wrote,

> ...everything exposed by the light becomes visible, for it is light that makes everything visible. This is why it is said: "Wake up, O sleeper, rise from the dead, and Christ will shine on you." Be very careful, then, how you live—not as unwise but as wise, making the most of every opportunity because the days are evil.

I knew the Lord was telling me something about myself and about other Christian women in America. He was saying, "Wake up from your ignorance and apathy about the world around you. Get up and get to work exposing the works of darkness around you! Use every opportunity available to defeat the devil and bring glory to God!"

When I first heard about the Houston convention, I knew that I had been guilty of being an uninformed

67

American. I was actively involved in the work of the church and spent years traveling with Tim giving Family Life Seminars, but by and large, I had remained unconcerned about the secular world and its problems.

What I know now is this: We Christians are not called by God to spend our lives doing "church" activities. The apostle Paul used military terminology to describe the life of every believer in Jesus Christ. We are soldiers in the army of the Lord here on this earth. And we are called to wage spiritual warfare against the principalities, powers, and authorities who are in opposition to our King, Jesus Christ.

Knowing that I am a soldier in a spiritual army has made it far easier for me to engage in the many and varied battles we've encountered. The Word of God tells us that we are not fighting against flesh and blood. We're not *really* in a battle against feminist leaders. We're engaged in a struggle against the spiritual forces of darkness that control these individuals.

I knew that if Concerned Women for America were to succeed against the immense political and economic power of the feminist movement and its allies, our traditionalist movement had to be based upon prayer. So, in August 1979, I appointed one of our founding board members to serve as our national prayer chapter director. It was her job to organize our members into powerful prayer chapters and to provide them with prayer concerns and ideas for constructive action.

To keep our women constantly up-to-date on threats to the family and to let them know of prayer needs, we sent out "Prayer/Action Alerts" each month to the prayer chapter leader. She then contacted members of her chain, and they agreed to pray about the issues we had given them. In order to include each member in the national network, we eventually incorporated the "Prayer Alert" into our monthly CWA newsletter.

In addition, we provide every CWA member with a card featuring the "Key 16 Prayer List," which names the sixteen political leaders who have ultimate authority over each individual in our society. Every member is encouraged to pray faithfully for these governmental leaders. We developed this list in obedience to Paul's command to Timothy in 1 Timothy 2:1-2 where he wrote, "I urge...that requests, prayers, intercession and thanksgiving be made for...all those in authority."

Our prayer chapter leaders are given wide latitude in the way they operate their chapters. We encourage the chapter members to meet together at least every other month to pray together and to work on specific educational activities. I am pleased to say that our committed women are involved not only at the federal level, but also at the local level.

In Jessup, Maryland, for example, a prayer chapter started to minister to the physical needs of the inmates of a nearby women's prison. At first, all these Christian women could do was send packages of writing paper, pens, and socks to the prisoners. Our CWA members prayed over these packages before they were dropped off at the prison. This process went on for more than a year before the warden of the prison finally allowed our ladies to meet the prisoners face-to-face.

Today, our CWA members are regularly praying with the women prisoners and sharing the gospel of Jesus Christ with them. CWA prayer chapters are actually springing up within the prison!

As I was going through my personal notes and old newsletters to prepare this book, I recalled one impressive example of the awesome power of prayer.

In the April/May 1982 issue of our CWA newsletter, I wrote the following:

> As I write, my heart is filled with unspeakable joy as I think back to the time when God gave me the burden to pray and fast every Wednesday. It had been an exhausting two weeks of traveling, and I was finally flying home. While reading some articles on the feminist commitment and their unlimited resources (which looked insurmountable), the ERA deadline of June 30 burdened me to pray.

I encouraged all of our members to begin praying every Wednesday, because the ERA deadline for ratification was on a Wednesday, June 30, 1982.

We began to see miracle after miracle occur on Wednesdays! On Wednesday, December 23, 1981, Idaho judge Marion Callister declared that the extended ERA deadline was illegally passed by Congress. He also declared that states could rescind their vote on the ERA!

On Wednesday, January 13, 1982, the Oklahoma senate defeated the ERA by a vote of 27 to 21. On the same day, the Illinois house proposed to drop the three-fifths majority vote needed for ratification to a simple majority. A straw poll in the Democratic caucus showed there were not enough votes to change the rules, so the ERA was not brought to a vote.

On January 19, the Oklahoma state senate again defeated the ERA by 27 to 21. On Wednesday, January 20, the Georgia house defeated the ERA by 116 to 57—a more than 2 to 1 margin of victory!

On Wednesday, February 3, the Virginia House Privileges and Elections Committee voted 12 to 7 against sending the ERA to the floor for a vote. On Wednesday, February 10, the Missouri State Constitutional Amendments Committee voted a 4 to 4 tie on the ERA, thus blocking passage.

We were thrilled when our research assistant compiled the information listed above. Out of nine votes, six had occurred on Wednesdays. And we had won them all! That's the power of prayer! The feminists may have access to the media, tax dollars, and the influence of notable personalities, but we have access to the Creator through fervent prayer!

Chapter 8

THE NEED FOR LEGAL DEFENSE

Concerned Women for America is a multi-faceted organization. We are not simply concerned about the feminist movement, but also about any movement that seeks to undermine or destroy the traditional family unit. More recently the battleground has centered around the education of our youth.

The women of Brazil discovered that Communists were using the educational system to brainwash their youngsters in Marxist doctrine. The same thing has happened in America. The humanists have used our educational system to preach their brand of anti-God, anti-American religious philosophy to our children. Christian women, like their counterparts in Brazil more than two decades ago, are rising in anger to oppose the subversives who seek to convert our children to Godless humanism.

As a result of this threat, one of our primary areas of interest is in public school education. We have long known that the humanists have seized control of our educational system and have been using the public schools to propagate the "religion" of humanism. Dedicated humanists such as John Dewey, the father of so-called "progressive education," have viewed the school system as the pulpit from which they can evangelize the youth of this nation. My husband goes into great detail about this serious problem in his book, *The Battle for the Public Schools*.

We know from our research and experience that the humanists look at the schools as a humanistic church, but I have never read a more candid admission of this fact than the statement of a young humanist intellectual named John Dunphy in the January/February 1983 issue of the *Humanist* magazine:

> I am convinced that the battle for humankind's future must be waged and won in the public school classroom by teachers who correctly perceive their role as the proselytizers of a new faith: a religion of humanity that recognizes and respects what theologians call divinity in every human being.... The classroom must and will become an arena of conflict between the old and the new— the rotting corpse of Christianity, together with all its adjacent evils and misery, and the new faith of humanism.... *It will undoubtedly be a long, arduous, painful struggle replete with much sorrow and many tears, but humanism will emerge triumphant* [Emphasis ours]. It must if the family of humankind is to survive.[1]

To make his point even more obvious he wrote to Jerry Falwell, advising,

> I would also strongly suggest that you bring this matter to the attention of your compatriots in the Christian Right; they, too, deserve to be informed of just what they are up against and I feel that my proposal of using public schools for the propagation of atheistic humanism should hold a considerable degree of interest for them.

Indeed, it has. You might want to reread his statements and let them sink in. It is the goal of humanism to use our public schools to brainwash our children into rejecting Christianity and embracing the religion of humanism. It is the objective of humanism to triumph over the "rotting corpse of Christianity." His statements also clearly demonstrate how necessary it is for pro-family groups such as CWA to establish legal defense foundations to defend our Constitutional rights. Dunphy and his cohorts are working day and night to stamp out any vestige of Christianity in America. We *must* defend ourselves.

CWA first became involved in waging legal battles against humanism back in 1980. Until then, we had no legal counsel in our employ and were not focused upon using the law and courts to obtain justice for persecuted Christians.

One afternoon Michael Farris, a young attorney from Spokane, Washington, called our office. He was one of the key lawyers involved in a lawsuit filed by four Washington state representatives to declare the illegality of the Equal Rights Amendment extension. Michael and his fellow lawyers felt that the ERA extension granted by Congress was an illegal act; they also believed it was permissible for states to change their minds about supporting the ERA.

The case was presented to Federal District Judge Marion Callister who ultimately ruled that the ERA extension was indeed unconstitutional and that the states did have the right to rescind their prior ratifications. But before this ruling could be made, Farris and the other lawyers had to fight a preliminary battle against religious bigotry.

Judge Callister is a devout Mormon. Because his church had actively opposed the ERA, the National Organization for Women attempted to have him thrown off the case. This was the first time in American history that a judge was attacked because of his religion.

In reponse to NOW's motion to disqualify the judge, Farris had filed a brief, pointing out that over fifty church organizations had taken a position one way or the other on the ERA. If Judge Callister was to be removed, then, in fairness, it could not be reassigned to a judge who belonged to Catholic, Presbyterian, Unitarian, Baptist, Methodist, or any of the other churches that had taken an opposing position.

In his brief Michael wrote, "In their lemming-like rush to see the ERA added to the Constitution, NOW not only perverts the constitutional process, but it threatens to drown the nation in a sea of religious bigotry." Former United States Senator Sam Ervin wrote Farris a letter congratulating him on his brief, which called NOW on the carpet for its religious bias. The federal courts denied NOW's motion, and Judge Callister went on to make his historic ruling.

NOW appealed the judge's decision to the United States Supreme Court. They expected and needed a quick victory. The Supreme Court denied their request for a quick reversal and placed the case on the ordinary calendar. After the extension period expired, the Supreme Court dismissed the case for mootness, being without legal significance.

We have since learned that Judge Callister's decision played an important part in defeating the ERA in many state legislative battles. In Georgia, the ERA opponents made no floor speeches against the ERA at all. They simply passed out copies of this decision, and the ERA was defeated by a two-to-one margin.

CWA's association with Michael Farris has proved to

be providential. Michael soon began serving as our legal counsel, traveling all over America for us. Now Farris and his family have moved to Washington, D.C., where he heads our lobbying office. He is a brilliant lawyer and a firmly committed believer in Jesus Christ. He is determined to see that Christianity is not stamped out in America. As a constitutional lawyer, he is working to preserve our religious freedoms as guaranteed under the United States Constitution. I believe he has been divinely appointed to serve as a defender of the rights of Christians.

Chapter 9

CAN A COURAGEOUS WOMAN BE SILENCED?

One of our greatest legal victories came against the National Education Association (NEA) in late 1983. For two years we had been engaged in a costly legal battle to defend a Tennessee mother and school teacher, Suzanne Clark, from an unjust lawsuit filed against her by the NEA.

The events surrounding the case began in January 1982 when Suzanne read an article entitled "Public Education Faces Threat," in the local paper, the *Bristol Herald Courier*. Written by Walt Mika, the president of the Virginia Education Association, and Terry Herndon, an NEA executive, it was a scathing attack on the Reagan administration for its education policies. These two educators argued that President Reagan and his political appointees were determined to wreck the public education system of America by promoting such "dangerous" concepts as abolishing the Department of Education, giving tuition tax credits to parents whose children were enrolled in private schools, and allowing prayer in school. After castigating the Reagan administration for these and other "sins," the authors stated, "What, after all, could be more cherished, wholesome and even innocent than public schools?"

Suzanne Clark was enraged when she read the article. She spent a couple of days preparing a well-documented rebuttal, which was printed in the Sunday paper, January 24, 1982, under the title, "So Much for Innocence: The Evils of the NEA."

Throughout her article, she quoted extensively from humanistic educators and from the NEA's own materials to show how morally subversive public school education is today. She pointed out that the NEA itself is on record as favoring a one-world government in its "Declaration of Interdependence: Education for a Global Community."

In its handbook, *Education for International Understanding in American Schools*, the NEA says, "the preservation of international peace and order may require that force be used to compel a nation to conduct its affairs within the framework of an established world system."[1]

The NEA also favors the use of drugs on school children. As Suzanne Clark observed,

> Still another cherished NEA innovation is the use of drugs such as amphetamines which are "useful tools," according to NEA official Sally Williams, "to aid in stabilizing the brains of children with learning disorders and hyperactivity. These drugs are unusually safe—much more than aspirin or penicillin." Yet FDA officials in Omaha warned against the use of two such drugs for "behavior modification."[2]

The NEA, said Mrs. Clark, is also promoting values-free sex education. Its recommended teaching methods are designed to "unfreeze" children from the "damaging" traditional values they receive at home. In addition, the NEA has gone on record supporting the "rights" of homosexuals to teach our youngsters. Wrote Suzanne

Clark, "...the NEA drafted resolutions in 1975 which included approval of homosexual teachers and said no person should be 'dismissed or demoted because of... sexual orientation.' "[3]

In closing, Suzanne Clark said,

> There is something sinister in the prediction made in an NEA journal, *Today's Education*, that schools "will be modified almost beyond recognition by the end of the century."

> That article went on to list as goals such things as: (1) Educators assuming responsibility for children when they reach age two; (2) Children being given drugs on an experimental basis; (3) Widespread busing of children; (4) Teachers becoming "learning clinicians," thus conveying the idea that schools are becoming clinics whose purpose is "to provide individualized psychosocial 'treatment' for the student...," i.e., mental healing, i.e., brainwashing.

> So much for innocence.[4]

Her article was well written and documented. But she had no idea it would cause such an uproar at NEA headquarters. Their attorneys contacted her by mail in March of 1982. In referring to her rebuttal, the attorneys said, "...you misstate NEA's position on various issues and cite in support of these misstatements sources that are inaccurate and untrue. Your column is so patently defamatory, and the errors so obvious, that we have no alternative but to conclude that your intent was to injure the good name and reputation of NEA." They insisted that she respond within fourteen days with a retraction or they would file a lawsuit against her.

She knew that what she had written about the NEA was true, so she refused to back down. "If I had signed the retraction," said Suzanne, "I suppose it would have been the easy way, but I couldn't do it in good conscience. I would have been lying and would have known I was lying."

The NEA lawyers then sued her for one hundred thousand dollars. The legal papers were delivered to Suzanne by a local sheriff. "When I was first served the suit, I had trouble eating and sleeping for three days," said Suzanne. "For an entire month, it was all so uncertain." She and her husband thought they would have to mortgage their home to defend themselves.

She called several different Christian organizations to see if they would help her, but none could come to her aid. When she contacted noted Christian attorney John Whitehead, he recommended she get in touch with Tennessee lawyer Larry Parrish, a former United States prosecutor who has earned a nationwide reputation for his antipornography victories. She took Whitehead's advice and found Parrish eager to take the case. Unfortunately, Suzanne had no funds to hire him.

During this emotionally draining experience, Suzanne, a CWA member, called our office for advice. Michael Farris recommended that we finance her defense against the NEA attack, and our board gave its unanimous approval. Our attorney became Larry Parrish's cocounsel in this important legal case. Both attorneys waged an aggressive case against the NEA. At a deposition, they forced top officials of the NEA to testify under oath about the NEA's role in promoting the nuclear freeze and sex education and to testify about their opposition to prayer in schools and the teaching of scientific creationism.

Parrish and Farris also obtained sworn testimonies from these officials about numerous noneducational activities: their support of the Equal Rights Amendment, federally funded abortion, and other issues. Some of the evidence against the NEA included tapes of the NEA board of directors laughing in derision at Suzanne and her religious principles. Under sworn testimony, the president of the NEA at the time admitted to Farris that the organization was at "war" with the "New Right," and that this lawsuit against Suzanne Clark was simply one "battle" in that war.

The case dragged on for more than a year until late in 1983 when the NEA decided to drop the case, just two weeks before the trial was to begin. This was a major victory for religious freedom! As Michael Farris remarked at the time,

> I think there are two reasons the NEA gave up. First, they were surprised to find Suzanne an articulate young woman who knew that she was telling the truth; and secondly, I think that they were totally surprised by the strength and vigor of our defense. This case has been a total embarrassment to the NEA, and I think that they were worried that a trial would only have served to embarrass them further.

The lawsuit was clearly designed to crush any opposition to the NEA's pro-humanist, pro-statist goals. When the NEA picked out Suzanne Clark of Bristol, Tennessee, for this attack, it figured it was just dealing with an uninformed "right wing" teacher from the Bible Belt. It planned to use her as an example to all others who might try to tell the truth about the NEA's activities. If it could silence her, it assumed it would have a chilling effect on others who might wish to expose the NEA.

The National Education Association has made it clear in its own public statements and printed materials that it is at war with the so-called "New Right." In a teacher training manual entitled "Combatting the New Right," published by the Western States Regional Staff of the NEA, it states,

> Throughout the nation's history, right wing extremists—racist, anti-civil rights, anti-labor, and anti-democratic—have played a recurrent role. In periods of economic and social change, these fringe organizations have often achieved fleeting success in exploiting the fears and frustrations of troubled Americans.[5]

The training manual then lists page after page of "right wing" organizations that are supposedly determined to destroy the public education system of America—and will drag America back into the Stone Age if not opposed. The manual also contains instructions on how teachers are to deal with "censors" who complain about the content of school textbooks.

The author then concludes,

> The NEA with its affiliates is the biggest, the most politically effective, and most powerful public employee organization of all. If they can defeat the NEA, the effort of all public employee groups to organize effectively will have been dealt perhaps a mortal blow; and, at the same time, the New Right will have had a major victory in its regressive stand on the issues that so vitally affect the quality of life in America.[6]

Concerned Women for America—through the sacrificial donations of thousands of women across America—provided more than seventy thousand dollars to defend

Suzanne Clark from an unfair attack against her by this powerful teacher's union.

We believe we have taught the NEA a hard lesson. And our CWA Education and Legal Defense Foundation is just as prepared today to defend the constitutional rights of those whose free speech is stifled.

Chapter 10

MOTHERS RISE UP AGAINST HUMANISM IN THE CLASSROOM

Even as the NEA was waging its legal battle against Suzanne Clark, other confrontations between the liberal education establishment and Christian parents were brewing elsewhere in the country. As a defender of religious liberty, CWA was being drawn into these battles as well.

In Spokane, Washington, a well-informed CWA member was embroiled in a controversy over the anti-Christian overtones of one of her daughter's high school literature books.[1] Carolyn Grove was protesting the use of a book called *The Learning Tree* in her daughter Cassie's English class. This assigned textbook was ostensibly about the life of blacks growing up in America during the 1920s, but in reality it denigrated Jesus Christ and Christian moral values.

The central character in this book is a twelve-year-old black boy who is caught in the path of a tornado. He is rescued by a nineteen-year-old prostitute who takes him into a slaughter house and seduces him on the floor. The author makes it clear that the tornado was caused by God, and leaves the impression that the young boy was far safer in the hands of a prostitute than God.

The tornado damages the local church, but by-passes the house of prostitution. Later in the book, this boy's brother-in-law, in a drunken state on a Sunday morning, starts shooting at heaven. He yells out, "I'm going to blow the a— off of Jesus Christ, that longlegged, white son-of-a-b——."

In another segment, his mother argues with her son about God and ends by remarking to her husband,

"He's a thinkin' boy, Jack. You should'a heard some of the questions he asked me about religion and death. I was hard put for the right answers, I'll tell you. It ain't just dyin' he wonders about. It's what comes after."

"He needs to go to church more, maybe."

"We've been goin' to church all our lives, and so has he; still hearin' the same things we been hearin' since we was his age. The answers that used to satisfy us ain't goin' to satisfy Newt and the young ones comin' up now. They want proof. Some kind they can see and feel. And they're goin' to want more out of this world than we're gettin' out of it. Time's changin', Jack."

In another section of the book, an older man sells "spots" under the bleachers at a baseball game for the little boys to look up women's dresses. Prices depend on whether the woman is wearing underwear or not.

When Cassie began reading this book as an assigned textbook, she was angered and hurt. The book was directly attacking her religious convictions, yet she was being *forced* to read it. Likewise, her mother was outraged when she learned that her daughter was being required to read blatantly anti-Christian books.

Carolyn studied the book in detail, and then asked the teacher if her daughter could be given an alternative reader. The teacher was agreeable to the suggestion and admitted that he was concerned over some of the objectionable material in the book, which had been chosen by his superiors.

He assigned Cassie *Puddin' Head Wilson* by Mark Twain. But, as he gave her the alternative reader, he stood in front of the class and said, "If any of the rest of you aren't strong enough to handle this book, you can ask for an alternate, too!"[2]

Cassie was also ridiculed in the school newspaper and suffered the taunts of non-Christians in the class. She was given an alternative reading, but the peer pressure was unbearable.

Carolyn Grove felt that if she did not fight to get the book removed altogether from the public school classroom, she would be guilty of aiding the humanists in their attacks against Christianity. Other children were involved, too. Other young minds were going to be poisoned by this book if she did not stand up for righteousness.

After intense prayer and counsel with her husband, she felt compelled to take action. The first step in her effort was to voice her objections to the vice-principal of the school. She explained why she was calling and asked him if he had ever read the book. He said no. She urged him to read it. Eventually she met face-to-face with the vice-principal, the principal, and the teacher.

She received no satisfaction from them. Her next step was to meet with the English department evaluation committee. Again, they were unanimous in their denial of her objections. The book was to stay.

After that she sought community support from both Christian and non-Christian friends in the area. When she presented the facts to these parents, they were invariably shocked and fully supported her efforts to get the book removed. They were ignorant of what their children were being taught!

At a school board meeting, more than three hundred people were present—both supporters and opponents. The teachers and many of the students declared their academic freedom to read the book. Carolyn had no objection to the students' reading the book. They could purchase the book or get a copy from the library. What she objected to was having the book as an *assigned textbook* for tenth graders. The book clearly violated the rights of all Christians. It was a direct attack on Jesus Christ, the Bible, and traditional morality.

Michael Farris first learned of Carolyn Grove's textbook controversy in a feature article written about her in the Spokane newspaper before he came to work for CWA. Through numerous conversations over the next few months, he took an interest in the case and was present at the school board meeting. He warned the school officials about the possible legal dangers of keeping the book in the class.

The press was also present at the meeting, and Carolyn Grove quickly learned how unfair the press can be. At one point in the meeting, Michael asked the superintendent of schools to read sections of the book for the press and the audience. The superintendent refused, but he asked a woman to read the passages. When the woman began reading, the TV reporter tapped the cameraman on the shoulder and he stopped taping. This happened twice during the meeting. It appeared that the press would not tape anything that was damaging to the school board.

Portions of the book were read to the parents present, however, and nearly all of them were aghast at what they were hearing. In fact, several parents decided that evening to remove their children from the school.

The school board, of course, voted unanimously against removing the book. That was when Michael Farris went to court, filing a lawsuit in federal court in Spokane, on New Year's Eve 1980. He demanded that the book be removed because it violated the constitutional requirement of religious neutrality in the public school systems. It was a direct attack on Christianity and promoted the religion of humanism.

He charged that it is not enough to offer an alternate reading. The peer pressure is simply too much to bear in such cases. It is unfair that only prayer and Bible reading be thrown out of the public schools. If there cannot be pro-religious materials, then there cannot be clearly anti-Christian materials, either.

Michael Farris believes that if the federal courts are going to throw pro-Christian activities out of public schools to "guarantee religious neutrality," then anti-Christian materials should be removed as well. But this is not happening. Christianity in particular is being singled out for attack in our school systems. *The Learning Tree* case is only one of many such cases. The Washington Education Association (WEA), the school district, and the American Civil Liberties Union were in opposition to Michael. The lawyer for the WEA (the state affiliate of the NEA) convinced the judge that the book did not violate religious neutrality, even though it called Jesus Christ a "white trash God" and a "longlegged white son-of-a-b——." The school lawyers convinced the judge that the case should be dismissed, which meant that Michael and Carolyn were denied a jury trial.

Carolyn asked Michael to appeal the case, but there was an urgent need to find financial backing for the appeal, which could end in the United States Supreme Court. That is when CWA began actively to support Carolyn's case.

The case is presently on appeal to the United States Court of Appeals for the Ninth Circuit in San Francisco. It is difficult to know how long it may be delayed. The case raises such important issues that it may ultimately be settled by the United States Supreme Court.

The central issue is not censorship of a book; it is an issue of coercion of conscience in violation of the principle of religious neutrality.

Vicki Frost and Public School Textbooks

Concerned Women for America has also decided to defend Mrs. Vicki Frost and her religious freedom in a similar textbook case in the state of Tennessee. Mrs. Frost of Church Hill was arrested in November 1983 and spent several hours in jail for the "crime" of trying to take her daughter out of a second grade class.[3]

A month prior to that, her daughter Sarah asked for help in answering a question from her reading book. The subject of this particular reading was occult telepathic powers. Vicki was stunned. She later discovered that information on occultic practices was included in a number of the readers used at the Church Hill Elementary School. Since Vicki has two other children who were also required to read those books, she studied the contents of the second, sixth, and seventh grade readers.

She immediately contacted other parents in the area to see if they were aware of what was being taught to their children. Most of the parents were uninformed, but when they read their children's textbooks, they were outraged!

Not only were their children—from the first grade through the eighth grade—being taught about occult practices, but they were also being taught about reincarnation, gun control, situation ethics, one-world government, socialism, evolution, and pacifism. In the sixth grade book, *Riders on the Earth* there are 130 pages dealing directly or indirectly with telepathic powers and how to develop and use this mind power. Scattered through each textbook are stories about eastern religions, spiritism, and poems or parables debunking Christianity. These books also sow the seeds of rebellion in the young by teaching them to question all authority and to make up their own moral standards.

Our attorney Michael Farris and his assistant examined all of these textbooks in detail. After their investigation, Farris concluded that the basic purpose of the textbooks is to train children to believe that all religions are the same in order to prepare these children for a new world order.

In his analysis of the texts, Farris observed, "It is important to note the great number of stories dealing very directly with religion. Chinese religious philosophy, American Indian spiritism and animism, Buddhism, Greek pantheism, Islam, and a great variety of other 'different' religions are presented."

There is not one positive story about Christianity in these texts. The general premise of the textbooks can be exemplified by a poem featured on page 408 of the book, *Great Waves Breaking*. The poem "The Blind Men and the Elephant" discusses six blind men who each bump into an elephant from a different direction. Each one describes what he thinks it is, but none is correct. One man described the elephant as a wall, and another said he thought it was more like a spear. Still another described it as a snake. The men made reasonable assumptions in their descriptions of the elephant, depending on which part they had been touching.

The whole point of the poem is summarized in the last two stanzas. The author, John Godfrey Saxe, claims that these blind men are like theologians who argue in "utter ignorance" about a God they have never seen. The theologians may all have a glimpse of the truth, but none is correct. Though each blind man thought he was right, "all were in the wrong."

This is only one example of literally hundreds of such stories in these readers published by Holt, Rinehart and Winston. Some of the other titles are: *People Need People, Freedom's Ground, Never Give Up, Special Happenings,* and *To See Ourselves.*

Vicki Frost studied these textbooks in detail. After spending much time in prayer with her husband, Vicki decided she would not allow her daughter to read any more pro-humanist or anti-Christian materials. Once she voiced her objections, the junior high principal allowed her children and a few others to read an alternative book. However, when the superintendent and the school board found out, they ordered the principal to expel all children in the sixth through eighth grades who objected to the books. The parents refused to compromise. The battle for religious freedom had begun.

Vicki and her friends protested against these textbooks to the local school board by forming a grassroots organization known as Citizens Organized for Better Schools (COBS). She and her allies were not requesting that the books be removed from school, only that their children be allowed to have an *alternate* textbook. She and her friends offered to serve as parent volunteers in the school to help their children with their reading, or to pay for a private tutor to help their children. None of these offers was accepted.

The COBS group withdrew their children from the reading classes. In retaliation, the school suspended these thirteen children for three days, hoping to force them back to school. When they returned, they still refused to read the texts. They were suspended for another ten days and then further suspended when they still refused to read the texts.

As the battle became uglier, school officials and other educators in the area made it clear to COBS that their children were no longer welcome in the public school system. The juvenile court system in Hawkins County soon became involved. Juvenile Judge Reece Gibson warned the parents that if they removed their children from the school, both parents and children could be arrested under truancy laws. Gibson, by the way, heads a group calling itself Citizens Advocating the Right to an Education, which is opposed to Vicki Frost and her supporters. Gibson's wife is also the vice-principal at the high school.

On November 23, Vicki Frost entered the principal's office at Church Hill Elementary School to ask that she be given permission to remove her daughter from the reading class. She was going to take her daughter to the school cafeteria to practice reading from another text.

Vicki sensed she might have trouble dealing with the principal, so she asked the chief of police to accompany her to the office to act as a witness. When she arrived at the office, the principal was unyielding and arrogant. She immediately charged her with trespassing and disrupting the school and demanded that she be arrested on the spot.[4]

Incredible as this may seem, the police chief *did* arrest

Vicki. She told him, "As long as you're going to arrest me, I'd like to take my child out of the classroom." The police chief grabbed her arm and told her, "You're the one who's going to jail, not your daughter."[5] He drove her twenty miles to the county jail in Rogersville, where she was fingerprinted, photographed, and locked in a jail cell.

Using her one phone call, Vicki alerted a friend to her dilemma and urged her to contact the CWA office in Washington, D.C. for help. Michael Farris had already been in contact with her before her jailing so he knew the constitutional issues involved.

His first job was to get her out of jail. He called the local judge and had Vicki freed within three hours. The police chief let her out of jail but did not provide any transportation for her back to Church Hill.

On December 2, 1983, Michael Farris, my husband, and I flew into Greeneville to hold a press conference, which formally announced our filing of a federal civil rights lawsuit against the school board, the principals of Church Hill Elementary School and Church Hill Middle School, Carters Valley Elementary School, and Mount Carmel Elementary School on behalf of Roger and Vicki Frost, their children, and the other families who were affected by the school's compulsive actions.

During our press conference, Michael Farris told reporters, "This is the first time an evangelical, fundamentalist group has been forced to court by the negative actions of a school district. We feel this is a landmark case."

In our lawsuit against the county schools, we asked the court to allow the suspended children to return to school and to require the county to provide alternate texts. We also sought an injunction prohibiting the schools from "compelling the student plaintiffs" to read anti-Christian books or from "taking adverse action against (students) for their refusal to read (the) books, including...any further suspension from school and the giving of any adverse grades for the work missed as a result of (the) suspension." We are also seeking monetary damages to pay for the schooling of these children.

Subsequently, Vicki Frost removed all four of her children from the public school system and enrolled them in a Christian school.

Michael Farris believes this case raises a serious constitutional question. He believes that the religious freedom of these parents is being blatantly violated by the school board. The Constitution guarantees us freedom of religion, yet these precious rights are being abridged when Christian children are compelled to read texts that are at odds with their values.

"It seems to me incongruous that kids who object to reading the Bible have all the rights in the world," Michael Farris noted, "yet the children who don't want to read these books don't have any rights at all." The press has remained relatively silent about this particular case, although several articles have accused Christians like Vicki Frost of trying to ban *Goldilocks and the Three Bears* from schools. *U.S. News & World Report*, however, in its February 20, 1984, issue, dealt briefly with her case and noted that this will be a "landmark" legal case.

In presenting his case before the United States District Court in Greeneville, Michael listed nine reasons why Christians should not be forced to read the Holt, Rinehart, Winston readers:

1. The books teach witchcraft and other forms of magic and occult activities. The Bible teaches that witchcraft, magic, and the like are of satanic origin and

are to be avoided by Christians.

2. The books teach that some values are relative, that is, the application of these values varies from situation to situation. Specifically, lying and stealing are taught as being relativistic values that are right sometimes and wrong sometimes. The Bible teaches that stealing and lying are always wrong.

3. The books teach attitudes, values, and concepts of disrespect and disobedience to parents. The Bible teaches that children are to honor and obey their parents.

4. The books depict prayer to idols, especially prayer to a Horse-god, which allegedly is the possible reason for the end of World War II. The Bible teaches that prayer to idols is sin and should never be practiced or countenanced in any way by Christians.

5. The books teach that one does not need to believe in God in a specific way but that any type of faith in the supernatural is an acceptable method of salvation. The Bible teaches that Jesus is the Way, the Truth, and the Life and that no man may come unto the Father except through Him.

6. The books describe a child who is disrespectful of his mother's activities in studying the Bible. The Bible teaches that such study of the Holy Scriptures is honorable and profitable for all, adults and children alike.

7. The books describe Jesus as being dependent upon Jewish scribes whom He distrusted as being necessary to "write his story" down on paper. Implied in this is that Jesus did not know how to read and write. The Bible teaches that the gospels (Jesus' story) were written by a tax collector, a physician, a fisherman, and a Greek preacher, not Jewish scribes. Furthermore, the Bible clearly teaches that Jesus could both read and write.

8. The books teach as fact that man has evolved from a common ancestor with various types of monkeys and that other facts support evolution as a fact. The Bible teaches that God created man in His own image on the Sixth Day of the literal creation week.

9. The books continuously and repeatedly teach values of the religion of humanism including self-authority, human resources for salvation, one-world concepts, antinationalism, and other matters that are the fundamental doctrines of the religion of humanism. By way of example, an article by Margaret Mead teaches that a second universal language is desirable. In this context, she teaches that God did not create all of the diverse languages. She also teaches that a one-world system is desirable. The Bible teaches that God is a jealous God and will not tolerate His children dabbling in other religions. Therefore, to read such stories constitutes dabbling in the religion of secular humanism, which is strictly forbidden by the Bible.

These are, simply stated, the reasons why Christian parents have refused to allow their children to read these books. Vicki Frost and these other Christian parents should be commended for the brave stand they have taken for righteousness and religious freedom in this country. Our nation, from its very inception, was founded by men and women who loved God and sought religious freedom for themselves.

Our government was founded upon an acknowledgment of God's sovereignty in the affairs of men. To deny religious freedom to these parents and children is to deny the very roots of our whole history as a free nation and to violate the clear protections of religious liberty spelled out in the Bill of Rights.

We are going to have more cases such as this one in

the future. I am convinced that the humanists are going to do everything they can to preserve the grim stranglehold they have on our children. They are the priests of religious humanism and are evangelizing our children for Satan.

We are going to oppose them, expose them, and defeat them whenever they threaten to corrupt our children with Godless philosophies and seek to destroy our religious liberties.

Chapter 11

THE INCREASING ASSAULT ON CHRISTIANITY

Suzanne Clark, Carolyn Grove, and Vicki Frost are three courageous women who have stood up against the humanistic educational establishment. Suzanne won her battle, but the others are still involved in costly litigation against the education bureaucracy.

CWA is not only continuing to defend the rights of Carolyn Grove and Vicki Frost, but our organization has also been involved in the controversial church-state dispute in Louisville, Nebraska.

This dramatic story began in 1977 when Pastor Everett Sileven opened an Accelerated Christian Education school in the basement of his tiny Faith Baptist Church in the farming community of Louisville. According to state law, Sileven violated statutes that require all schools—both religious and secular—to follow state guidelines on curriculum and teacher certification.

The state of Nebraska demanded that Sileven's Christian school, which was an integral part of their church ministry, 1) be licensed by the state, 2) limit the number of books concerning "religion and philosophy" in the school library to 2 percent of the collection, and 3) hire only "certified" teachers from state-approved colleges. In order to comply with Nebraska laws, Sileven would have to meet at least eighty-two different regulations, which stipulated everything from the age of textbooks to the kinds of courses taught. The state would also have control over course *content*.

Pastor Sileven refused to abide by these laws, claiming that the state had no right to interfere with his ministry. Yet Nebraska education bureaucrats continued to push the issue. Sileven was arrested and spent four months in jail. The battle has been raging for the seven years since then. In October 1982, a district court ordered the church padlocked so the school would not be used.

By September 1983, Sileven had gained so many allies that he openly defied state authorities and reopened the school. Judge Ronald Reagan, a district court judge, issued a contempt citation against Principal Sileven and seven of the parents who were sending their children to the school. The parents had the reasonable fear that if both father and mother of each family were jailed, the judge would order their children to become wards of the state and placed in foster homes.

Reagan appeared to ignore state laws and the United States Constitution in the action against Faith Baptist Church. On November 23, 1983, he ordered the seven fathers to appear in court to testify about Faith Christian School and their involvement in it.

They refused to say anything, claiming protection under the Fifth Amendment to the Constitution, which says a person cannot be forced to testify against himself. Another point should be made: these parents were not a party to any legal case pending in that court. They were jailed but were never even charged with any crime.

Concerned Women for America did not get involved in this legal case until the parents were arrested. Until that time we simply watched the developments and assumed that Pastor Sileven had competent legal counsel.

After the fathers were arrested and their wives and children were forced to flee the state because of a warrant for their arrest, we went to their defense. But Judge Reagan would not read Michael Farris's legal briefs, nor would he allow the fathers to come into the courtroom to attend some of their own hearings.

In January 1984, Civil Rights Commission Chairman Clarence Pendleton visited Nebraska. Pendleton remarked to the press that he hoped this religious freedom issue wasn't going to be the civil rights movement of the 1980s. He acknowledged the fact that there were some civil rights problems, but he refused to become involved.

We should inform Clarence Pendleton that religious persecution *is* the civil rights movement of the 1980s, and we may just have to be as militant in demanding our religious freedoms as the blacks were in demanding their rights in the 1960s. We are demanding justice!

The Nebraska case is only one of many such cases that deserve our attention. The fathers were released from jail on February 23, 1984, after they agreed to keep their children out of Faith Christian School. But many of the men's lives are ruined. They are reunited with their wives and children, but some of them lost their jobs. Why? Because they wanted to educate their children in a Christian school.

The Coming Religious Persecution

There are some very basic principles involved in the Nebraska case and others like it. The issues of religious freedom and the so-called separation of church and state, however, have been deliberately confused by those who demand freedom for everyone but Christians.

Where do you draw the line between proper government authority and a violation of religious liberty? Michael Farris believes the state can interfere with church business only if there is a clear and present danger to public health or safety. Otherwise, the government is to keep its hands off church activities.

The state can legitimately concern itself with health, safety, and sanitation standards, but it has no authority to dictate to a Christian school what its curriculum will be; nor must it dictate qualifications for teachers. In the Nebraska case, there was no argument over the quality of education the children were receiving. These children regularly scored from one to three years ahead of children who were attending accredited state run schools. The issue was over unrestrained control of curriculum and teachers.

The church and Christians are increasingly under attack. New issues are being raised which will inevitably restrict our religious freedoms—unless we resist. Can zoning laws, for example, be used to prohibit Bible study groups from meeting in private homes? Can the government force Bible schools to admit homosexuals, alcoholics, or drug addicts? Can the states legally control the curricula of Christian schools? Is it a violation of the supposed principle of separation of church and state for Christian students to pray together in public school?

Not only are these questions being raised, but the Internal Revenue Service has taken an activist role in harassing churches and parachurch ministries (Congressman George Hansen's book, *To Harass Our People*, gives a thorough discussion of the IRS's dictatorial powers).

How did we come to this point? Are we really supposed to be a secular state? Should the church confine its activities to socials and songfests instead of actively confronting a corrupt world?

Our nation has drifted toward an amoral, God-hating, secular state because we Christians have been ignorant of the enemies' devices. We have been uninformed not only about current events, but also about the rich religious history of this great nation.

America Was Founded on Christian Principles

The men and women who first colonized this nation came here seeking religious freedom from the persecution of the state-sanctioned Anglican church in England. The Pilgrims, who were labeled as separatists, fled from England and spent a dozen years in Holland before emigrating to America.

When they came to this country, they set up their own "state church" and began persecuting others who did not worship as they demanded. The Puritans did not tolerate dissension either.

Roger Williams, a preacher who lived in the Massachusetts Bay Colony, was soon to challenge the Puritans. He was apparently so driven by his desire to be doctrinally pure that he alienated his fellow Separatist pastors. He went so far as to argue that the king of England had no right to grant Indian lands to the colonists. Using this logic, he held that the Puritans had no legal authority to impose their religious views on those who arrived in the New World. He felt that all people should have the freedom to worship God as they wished—and not be coerced into obeying the doctrines of a particular denomination.

Williams's beliefs were viewed as outrageous and subversive by the Puritan leaders. As a result, he was forced to flee to what is now Rhode Island, where he founded the city of Providence as a haven for those who wished to worship God as they saw fit. From bitter personal experience, Williams knew the danger of living under a church-state. He promoted the concept of liberty of conscience, and granted religious freedom to all who wished to live in Providence.

Williams was viewed as a dangerous radical by the Puritan hierarchy, but his view of religious liberty was eventually embodied in the First Amendment to our Constitution.

When the founding fathers came together to write the Constitution and Bill of Rights, they were mindful of the potential tyranny of a church-state. They were *not*, however, *against* state churches. In discussing the Constitution, Michael Farris has written, "The historically accurate view of the First Amendment is not that the founders feared mixing religion and government, rather they feared federal control of their state religion and governmental mix."

This is why they knew it was vital to draft a document that would protect the religious liberty of all Americans from federal encroachment, regardless of their religious beliefs. That is why the First Amendment specifically prohibits *Congress* from establishing a state church. It does not, however, prohibit the states from having state-sanctioned churches.

In fact, at the time the Bill of Rights was written, nine of the thirteen colonies still had state churches. Massachusetts, for example, paid the salaries of its Congregational ministers until as late as 1833. And forty-seven of the fifty-two signers of the Constitution were members of one of these state-established churches. These men were determined to keep the federal government from destroying the religious liberties of all Americans.

"The intent of the First Amendment was simply to keep the Federal government out of the arena of religion and to keep away from a nationally established church," Michael Farris has written. "In no sense was the First Amendment an attempt to secularize public institutions or forbid church or religious involvement in politics. It was purely and simply a measure to keep the Congress off the back of the church. The reverse was not prohibited."

In March 1984, the Supreme Court dealt with one serious issue of church-state relationships. The Court ruled five to four that a city may display a nativity scene during the Christmas season without violating the so-called separation of church and state. The Court opinion, written by Chief Justice Burger, clarified the term *wall of separation* (between church and state) by noting that it was not a "wholly accurate description of the practical aspects of the relationship that in fact exists." The Constitution does not require a total separation of church and state, but, says Burger, it "affirmatively mandates accommodation, not merely tolerance, of all religions, and forbids hostility toward any."

Although this has been a victory for the cause of religious freedom, much more needs to be done to restore this nation to a reliance on biblical principles.

The founding fathers feared a national church, and so do I. But they realized that religious principles cannot and must never be separated from our personal morality or from the laws governing our nation. All laws are based upon someone's moral values. In England and North America our whole legal systems have been based upon Christian principles, yet these principles are now under attack by the secular humanists.

George Washington, in his Farewell Address, told us of the importance of adhering to Christian morality in government:

> Of all the dispositions and habits which lead to political prosperity, Religion and Morality are indispensable supports....And let us with caution indulge the supposition that morality can be maintained without religion....reason and experience both forbid us to expect that national morality can prevail in exclusion of religious principle.[1]

Under our Constitution, written by men who believed in a Supreme Creator, we are to be protected from the oppression of tyrannical manmade laws. The government is to be a servant of man, not his master. The Constitution does not *grant* us rights, but *protects* our God-given rights to life, liberty, and the pursuit of happiness.

Our nation has been prosperous and a blessing to every other nation on the earth because we have been motivated and ruled by Christian principles. Our nation has survived because we believed in the importance of *self-control*.

James Madison once wrote,

> We have staked the whole future of American civilization, not upon the power of government, far from it. We have staked the future of all of our political institutions upon the capacity of mankind for self-government, upon the capacity of each and all of us to govern ourselves, to control ourselves, to sustain ourselves according to the Ten Commandments of God.[2]

The only reason our republic—and personal freedom—have survived for two hundred years is that they were founded on Christian principles. As James Madison noted, self-government is possible only when men and women yield themselves to the control of God. If they are not controlled by a "higher law" (the commandments of God), then they will invariably succumb to their sinful natures.

If the Christians of this nation are ever driven underground, there will be no spiritual influence to hold back the natural tendencies of man. Human history is filled with examples of bloody wars that have been fought, not only by anti-God forces, but also by religious bigots who were unwilling to grant others the same freedoms they wished for themselves. Witness the terrible bloodbath that has occurred in Iran since the Ayatollah Khomeini seized power. His "religious beliefs" have created a terror-filled dictatorship, just as evil and merciless as any Communist regime.

"Public Policy" against Religious Freedom

Our nation is unique because *all* religious viewpoints are granted equal protection under the United States Constitution—or they were until recently. We have successfully avoided the bloody religious wars that ravaged Europe in times past because we all once believed in religious freedom.

Times are changing, however. The secularists have been cleverly using the First Amendment to suppress religious freedom. One of the most blatant examples of this suppression in recent years involves Bob Jones University.

On May 23, 1983, the Supreme Court of the United

States ruled that the Internal Revenue Service was correct in removing the tax-exempt status of BJU because the university forbade interracial dating or marriage. This school policy was based upon their particular interpretation of Scripture. We may disagree with this policy, but that's not the issue. The point is this: Should the Internal Revenue Service have the power and authority to punish a religious educational institution because its racial policies differ from those of the IRS?

The Internal Revenue Service contended that BJU's racial views violated "public policy" against discrimination. This was a cleverly concocted case. A whole new concept has been introduced into our legal system with this Bob Jones decision. The concept of public policy can now be used as a blanket indictment of *any* religious practice which may be held to violate "public policy."

A more recent case in point involves the city of New York and the Salvation Army. Each year, the city donated hundreds of thousands of dollars to the Salvation Army to help this Christian organization feed, house, and clothe hundreds of derelicts and street people. New York, however, has just withdrawn its support from the Salvation Army. Why? Because New York City has a public policy that prohibits discrimination against homosexuals. The Salvation Army rightfully views homosexuality as a serious sin and refuses to change its scriptural viewpoint. So who is going to suffer? The poor, the crippled, the blind—those the liberals in New York City claim to love so much!

The concept of public policy is dangerous to religious freedom since public policy is a constantly changing thing, barely definable. It means whatever the bureaucrats wish it to mean. If, for example, it becomes public policy for homosexuals to be granted legal sanction as a minority, there is nothing to keep the bureaucrats from *requiring* churches, Christian schools, or the Boy Scouts to hire a certain quota of homosexuals.

Carried to extremes, the public policy concept could be even more frightening. For instance, certain psychiatrists in this country contend that it is comforting and beneficial for preteen-agers if the fathers have intercourse with them. What if those psychiatrists' views somehow became public policy?

Organizations of pedophiles (child molesters) are lobbying for the legalization of sex with children. The Guyon Society, for example, has as its motto, "Sex Before Eight or Else It's Too Late." And the North American Man-Boy Lovers Association is pursuing the same goals. In early 1984, the homosexuals welcomed these child molesters into their movement. Now that the pedophiles are part of a perverse political movement, we shouldn't be surprised to see a push for public policy changes in our child protection laws. The threat to our children is real!

Will you someday be guilty of child abuse if you *don't* have sex with your children? This is not an absurd proposition. Twenty years ago who would have thought that it would be legal to kill your unborn baby or let your handicapped infant starve to death on a cold steel shelf in a hospital? Who would have dreamed there would be a Hemlock Society, a California-based group seeking to legalize suicide? With these and other corrupt practices going on in our society, why should we be surprised if incest were someday given legal protection as public policy?

1980s—The Battle for Religious Freedom

We may not wish it were so, but this decade is going to continue to be one of increased religious persecution in America. It is not enough simply to remain in our churches, doing the comfortable things we enjoy. We are involved in a life-and-death struggle against the power of the state. If we lose this struggle, our children will become wards of the state, our religious liberties will be restricted to within the walls of our churches, our access to the media will be cut off, the taxation of churches will increase, and the state religion of humanism will grow more and more intolerant as the years pass.

We have a choice to make. Will we submit to state tyranny or will we stand up and cry, "We will obey God, rather than men," regardless of the consequences?

Chapter 12

CWA STANDS AGAINST LEGALIZED MURDER

When a twelve-year-old girl nearly died after a doctor performed a late-term abortion, CWA entered the case. One of Michael Farris's first cases on behalf of CWA came to be known as the "Florida Abortion Case."

This child had gone to two different abortion clinics, but was refused because she was so late in her pregnancy. She persisted, however, and found a doctor who agreed to abort the child for one thousand dollars. In the operating room, the doctor tried to perform a suction abortion on the fully developed seven-month-old unborn child.

His first try only succeeded in sucking the baby's brain out. Then he tried to remove the remains of the baby with instruments, but only tore off the left arm and right leg.

In the process of trying to scrape this once-living unborn infant from the girl's womb, the doctor punctured her uterus and damaged her intestinal tract beyond repair. She began bleeding profusely and went into shock. She was rushed by ambulance to the nearest hospital, where a team of ten physicians worked for hours to save her life. They had to remove the remains of her dead child and then perform a hysterectomy and colostomy.

Janet Reno, the prosecuting attorney for Dade County (Miami) Florida, courageously charged the doctor with three crimes: assault with a deadly weapon for hurting the girl, violation of Florida's late-term abortion law, and most importantly, common law homicide for killing a human being.

When Michael Farris heard of this horrifying incident, he decided to file an *amicus* (friend of the court) brief, supporting the homicide charges against the doctor for killing an unborn, fully developed child. Michael was not the primary prosecutor in the case, but his extensive *amicus* brief explained what the Florida legislators were intending to do when they wrote the late-term law.

In his brief, Michael Farris observed,

Concerned Women for America...contends that the most fundamental area of protection that must be extended to unborn children is the right to live, which is meaningful only if it is protected by the homicide statutes. It makes no sense to extend some civil rights to persons but to refuse to recognize their most fundamental right to live.

The case was important for two reasons. First, no state law outlawing late term abortions had ever been upheld when challenged in the courts. Second, by charging the doctor with the crime of homicide, the prosecutor was raising the possibility of a higher court reversing *Roe* v. *Wade* by ruling that abortions are murders.

The trial judge agreed with CWA's arguments and upheld the constitutionality of the late term abortion law. CWA's lawyer discovered that the code reviser in charge of organizing the laws into the statute books had mixed-up Florida's late-term abortion law with another law regulating abortion clinics. The trial judge attached some of our research to his opinion to demonstrate that when the laws were properly understood, they were constitutionally valid. This was the first time any court had upheld a law prohibiting late-term abortions.

The judge did rule, however, that it was unconstitutional to charge the doctor with the crime of homicide (manslaughter). The prosecutor has appealed, and CWA has filed an *amicus* brief supporting this charge.

CWA is the only organization that has been involved on either side of this case. There were no pro-abortion groups or other pro-life groups involved.

Michael was pleased with the outcome, but is anxious to have the appellate courts rule on the legal issues of whether an unborn child is a "person" with rights guaranteed under the Constitution. In his appeals brief, he has presented a clear argument defending the rights of the unborn, comparing the status of the unborn to the status of blacks until the middle of the nineteenth century.

At that time, under the common law, "...it was not a homicide to kill a black slave, because black slaves were not considered human beings for legal purposes." We know now, of course, that the law was wrong to permit blacks to be killed as nonpersons under the Constitution. Yet we now abide by the Supreme Court decision of 1973, which says that unborn children are not worthy of protection.

The laws, however—both federal and state—are inconsistent when dealing with the unborn. Farris pointed out that "unborn viable children are winning increasing recognition of their civil rights. Both state and federal courts have adopted an increasingly compassionate attitude towards the rights of unborn children in many contexts." In many state cases, unborn children are defined as "human beings" for legal purposes in wrongful death actions. In other instances, they are given the right to be saved by medical means if an abortion fails.

In California, there was a grisly example of legal inconsistency in the case of a woman whose husband accused her of becoming pregnant by another man. He said he was going to kill her unborn child by "stomping" it out of her, which he proceeded to do. The California Supreme Court ruled that such a vicious act of murder was not a crime in the state because the legislature had failed to specifically outlaw feticide (the killing of a fetus).

So in one state an unborn child is defined as a "human being" while in another the child is defined as a "fetus," which has no rights whatsoever. Our legal system is no better than the one that functioned under Adolf Hitler. The Nazis justified the killing of senile old persons, the handicapped, and eventually entire races of people by simply changing the definitions of "person" in the laws. Under Nazi law, Jewish people were "nonpersons" who were devoid of rights. Therefore, it was perfectly legal to gas them, incinerate them, bulldoze them into lime pits.

I believe Almighty God is going to pour out His wrath on this nation if we do not, once again, protect the right of the unborn. We cannot continue to kill 1.5 million unborn babies a year and think that God will bless this nation. We cannot sit by while liberal judges distort the law to suit their own preconceived relativistic ideas.

Our nation must return to an uncompromising belief in the existence of God! And if God exists, then we must again create laws that conform to His revealed Word, the Bible. We must work to return Judeo-Christian morality to our legal system. Human freedom will not long survive if the law degenerates into a relative concept, determined by opinion polls, or the whims of nonelected humanistic judges.

We are already justifying the killing of the unborn and of handicapped infants. We have redefined them as "nonpersons" under the law. Is it so farfetched to believe we will one day be murdering races or classes of people? Will a Constitution protect us when judges ignore it—with impunity?

Our nation has sinned greatly since 1973. More than 15 million babies have been brutally murdered in hospitals and abortion mills. We are often shocked to see photographs of Nazi concentration camps. We cringe when we gaze upon the mountains of flesh being bulldozed into the lime pits.

Yet the slaughter of baby humans goes on in secrecy within our medical centers. The aborted babies are dumped in trash cans or shoveled into ovens for cremation. We feel self-righteous in our hatred of the Nazi death camps. But are we so much more noble than the Nazis? There are no piles of dead babies to look at; there are no concentration camps filled with dying children in America. But the deaths are all around us.

Until enough concerned Americans rise up in anger against the legalized murder of unborn children, this holocaust will continue unabated.

Legal protection for the right to life must begin from the moment of conception. No other option is possible if we truly believe in the sanctity of human life.

Chapter 13

CHRISTIAN WOMEN MOVE ON CAPITOL HILL

September 27, 1983, was an exhilarating, victorious day for me and for thousands of Christian women all across this land, for it was the day that Concerned Women for America officially opened its Washington, D.C., office.

I really believe this was a historic occasion for Bible-believing Christian women. Why? Because it is the first time in recent history that these Christian women have had serious, full-time representation in the nation's capital, where so many policies are made that affect our lives.

If you believe in the sanctity of the home and the importance of applying Christian principles not only in daily life but also in government, then CWA is there in Washington to represent you.

In Washington we have a competent staff of lawyers and assistants to defend the rights of Christian women from government encroachment. We are there to make our views known to the Congress.

The more I traveled around the country meeting with Christian women and discussing the pressing issues facing this nation, the more obvious it became that we had to have representation in Washington, D.C.

That conviction was confirmed time and time again. And as we began to work more with Michael Farris, he told us that it was essential we get an office in Washington. It was imperative that we have at least one person to lobby and keep us informed on current legislation. We also needed someone there to attend hearings in both the Senate and the House when important family-related legislation was being considered. (Until we had the resources, we had to rely on other conservative groups in Washington to keep us informed—the publications and staffs of the Free Congress Research and Education Foundation, The Right Woman, and the Eagle Forum.)

We prayed and planned for more than two years before the Washington office finally became a reality. But until we made definite plans for the fall of 1983, nothing had opened for us. It was a step of faith. As soon as we had committed ourselves, however, the Lord began putting everything together. We quickly located an office within walking distance of the Capitol Building. The rent was reasonable and the building was in a relatively safe area. In addition, Michael Farris's move from Washington state was going smoothly. We felt God's approval on our efforts. All the pieces of our puzzle were falling into place. The Lord had blessed our step of faith!

Before launching into a new project as monumental as this, we realized we should ask our CWA members what they thought about the idea. I sent out a letter to everyone on our mailing list, asking for their opinions. The response was overwhelming—and nearly unanimously—positive! They loved the idea! I knew in my heart that the Lord had given us the green light.

Michael Farris, our official representative in Washington, was given the task staffing our office. He contacted an ex-feminist who had received Christ several years ago and had been doing a superb job with our state representative in Maryland, Mary Jane Wright.

Our grand opening was held on September 27, 1983. That morning, we held a press conference with approximately thirty members of the Washington press corps.

"This opening is an event our approximately two hundred thousand members and supporters have long-awaited," I announced. "But it is more than a physical act; we believe that the opening of this office also sends out a message—a message that needs to be heard by the Administration, by Congress, by the media, and by the American public.

"And this is our message: *The feminists do not represent all women of America. The women of this country are every bit as pluralistic as the men.*

"It is the height of absurdity to suggest that all women are in a lockstep march led by Betty Friedan and Gloria Steinem. This suggestion is not only absurd, but, ultimately, it is also nothing more than recycled sexism to suggest that 'all women' follow the liberal ideology touted by the feminists.

"The feminists demand abortion rights on demand. Millions of women believe in the sanctity of human life and the rights of the unborn to live.

"The feminists fight for the passage of the Unisex Insurance Rates bill, which would be a financial liability to most women. This would cost them hundreds of dollars more each year without providing them with measurable benefits. Millions of women view this as unfair and oppose it.

"The feminists have strongly supported the nuclear freeze movement. They do not represent those millions

121

of women who believe that the Russian Communists cannot be trusted and that we need a strong military defense.

"We women are pluralistic. Women speak with many voices. Concerned Women for America is here in Washington to end the monopoly of the feminists who claim to speak for all women.

"There has been much talk lately regarding a gender gap between women and the Reagan Administration. We believe the gender gap is really a hoax. Millions of women voted for Ronald Reagan because of his strong stand on traditional moral values. Without the support of these women he would not have been elected. All too often the Administration and other government leaders hear only from the feminists who usually oppose those values.

"We believe the time has come for our government leaders to hear from the majority of the women in this country. Concerned Women for America is a rapidly growing organization of nearly two hundred thousand members from all walks of life. They are homemakers, single parents, married women, college women, career women, professional women, and retired women. In a pluralistic society, their views—far more in line with the views of most of America's women—deserve to be heard.

"We think it is time for all women to be heard. Let America understand that we will not be represented by a voice with which we do not agree."

The press conference went as you might have expected. Although over thirty representatives from various TV stations, newspapers, and magazines showed up, very little appeared in the press the following day.

USA Today and *The Washington Times* gave us some good coverage, but by and large our appearance on Capitol Hill was blacked out by the major media sources.

By the end of the press conference, we were looking forward to a relaxing lunch. Unfortunately, a brash *Washington Post* reporter failed to arrive on time for the press conference and talked me into giving her a private interview.

I was not quite prepared for her hostility. It became obvious that she had no intention of writing a fair story. In fact, it appeared to me from her hostile attitude that she only desired to vent her bias against Christian principles. She didn't interview me. She badgered and argued with me for two hours, and made me miss my luncheon engagement. What's worse, after she had wasted two hours of my time, she didn't print one word about the CWA opening in the *Washington Post*. So much for objective reporting.

For several years the phrase "the Silent Majority" was a press term used to describe traditional Americans who favor morality and decency in government. The truth is that we are not silent and haven't been for years. However, the press has made us "the Silenced Majority" by ignoring us.

The open house, later in the evening, proved to be a blessing for all of us. We had over two hundred guests from conservative and Christian organizations, plus aides from Senators' and Representatives' offices. During the whole three-hour celebration, the place was literally packed as more and more guests came and went. Our friends had given us a warm welcome, and the press corps had, in general, blacked us out. But we were now firmly established in Washington, D.C., as the voice for

Bible-believing Christian women.

The 535 Program

With our new office in Washington, we are better equipped to keep our members informed on legislative matters. But we are also acutely aware of the need to let our legislators know how many conservative Christian women of America feel about current legislation affecting the stability of the family.

In order to effectively lobby or influence the content of legislation on Capitol Hill, we came up with a new concept—one that has probably never been implemented in quite this way. We call it the 535 Program. Through CWA, we train women to become lobbyists for pro-family causes. One woman is assigned to each of the 435 representatives in Congress. In addition we have one hundred women representing Christian women in the Senate. These are our Capitol Hill congressional liaisons. They will become regular visitors at their congressmen's office, checking on current legislation and letting the congressmen know of our views.

In addition, we are training an equal number of women to serve as home district congressional liaisons. These women are serving the same function in the congressman's home district. By working together, the women on Capitol Hill and those in the home districts will monitor current legislation, give us updated information on how each congressman is going to vote, and provide the congressman with our viewpoint on moral and social issues. Our home district liaisons will also work closely with CWA prayer chapter leaders to pray and act on specific legislative issues. Who but a woman has the time, energy, and determination to accomplish such a positive task for our nation?

In addition, as an aid to our CWA members who are becoming involved in the political process, we have published a pamphlet called, "How to Lobby from Your Kitchen Table," which has been distributed by the hundreds of thousands. In a very simple, straight forward way, we have explained how a woman can take an active role in changing the course of history. That may sound somewhat overstated, but it's not. Sitting at her kitchen table, a woman can prepare well-reasoned letters that will affect the voting patterns of our elected officials. Furthermore, by writing letters to the editors of magazines and newspapers, as well as to advertisers, a woman can respond to the issues that are of concern to her.

It only takes a few minutes, a pen and paper and accurate information to generate an effective letter to a legislator. We encourage women to subscribe to our monthly CWA newsletter so they can get accurate information. Our representatives in Congress recognize that one letter from a constituent actually represents the views of more than one hundred other people who didn't have the discipline to write.

That's why it is so important for you to keep in constant touch with your United States senators and representatives, and your state legislators as well. You are blessed to be living in a nation where your voice, your opinions *do* matter. You elect these men and women to represent you. They can't do an effective job if they never hear from you. If you would like a free copy of our pamphlet, "How to Lobby from Your Kitchen Table," or wish to obtain more information about CWA, just write to Concerned Women for America, P.O. Box 5100, San Diego, California 92105.

I am convinced that we can turn this nation around, but we can only do it through the unbeatable combination of prayer and action. Through CWA, we have provided the leadership for the Christian women of America to be involved in a history-changing movement.

Chapter 14

CWA TAKES A GIANT STEP OF FAITH

In the fall of 1983, the Lord began to show me how we could use television to get our pro-family message to a much wider audience than we had been reaching so far. On separate occasions, two media experts visited our San Diego office. One man suggested we do an hour-long, prime time documentary telling the dramatic story of CWA. The second man, from Victory Communications, told us how we could use satellite technology to communicate directly with thousands of our CWA members. Through his firm, we could set up a live meeting in Washington, D.C., and then broadcast it via satellite all over America to as many conference halls as we could afford.

I was thrilled at the prospect of doing both projects, but reality soon set in. I knew we didn't have the time, money, or resources to produce a documentary *and* a teleconference, which would cover more than one hundred cities. That weekend I prayed for guidance and struggled to find the Lord's leading in this matter. Once the decision seemed clear, we met again with the representative from Victory Communications to begin hammering out some concepts.

As we prayed and talked, God gave us five purposes

for holding a national convention:

1. To present a moral, spiritual, and political platform for Christian women in this crucial election year.

2. To unite the Christian women through a network of prayer and action.

3. To inform our members of the most recent legal and legislative activities of CWA in protecting the rights of the family.

4. To make a public statement to the press and to the country that Christian women will be involved in setting the agenda on women's issues because we represent the majority viewpoint.

5. To strengthen our numbers by recruiting new members.

This is the biggest challenge CWA has ever taken on! The national convention is going to be a "coming out" party for the Christian women of this nation. It is time we made a public statement to the entire nation that the feminists do not speak for all the women of America, only for a handful of dissident women who have been deluded into following Marxist sloganeering. Yet because of the feminists' brashness and arrogance, they have managed to gain media coverage. That monopoly is coming to an end. The people of this nation will realize that the majority of women in America are not in favor of lesbianism or one-world socialism.

This "coming out party" will be held at the Shoreham Hotel in Washington, D.C., on September 14 and 15, 1984. On the first day we have invited President Ronald Reagan to address women's issues. We will also be featuring short video documentaries telling of our legal victories.

At the convention, twenty-four hundred of our members in attendance will hear messages from dynamic

Christian leaders on the moral, spiritual, and political platform of CWA. And the closing "Praise Celebration" will be broadcast live, via satellite, to more than one hundred cities. During this celebration, we will replay President Reagan's speech from the previous night.

One of the most important events of the convention will be our prayer meeting, which will link our CWA members together in what may very well be the largest televised prayer meeting in history. We're going to get on our knees, twenty-four hundred of us in Washington, D.C., and thousands more in convention halls throughout America.

In response to 2 Chronicles 7:14, we are going to repent of our sins together; we're going to ask God to bless our leaders with wisdom and strength; and we're going to call upon our heavenly Father to defeat His enemies!

We have made plans to tape the entire event and make a documentary from it for rebroadcast at a later date. By choosing to hold the national convention, we are also able to get the documentary I was hoping to produce! God has worked out every detail!

Through this convention, it could be that the Lord is going to use women to turn the tide in this nation. Godly women, gathered for prayer, cannot help but have a lasting impact for righteousness.

The Future of CWA

As the Lord leads, we are going to develop a network of Christian lawyers throughout the nation who will work together to counteract the actions of such groups as the American Civil Liberties Union. We will aggressively pursue legal cases wherever there is a threat to religious freedom or the rights of the family. Ours will not always be a defensive fight; we are already on the offensive.

For decades the liberals and radicals have enjoyed a monopolistic hold on our legal system. They have used the judicial system to destroy religious freedom and human rights, and have coddled criminals and sanctioned the murder of unborn babies. We seek justice in the legal system, and we will have it.

We are going to produce a series of prime time television documentaries, either telling about our own activities or exposing the evil activities of such groups as the ACLU, People for the American Way, Planned Parenthood, and others. Ours is a crusade to protect this nation from the most dangerous religion in the world: secular humanism. We will do it through pamphlets, books, television, seminars, videotapes, and conventions. We will use whatever communications tools are available to disseminate the *truth* to the American people. In addition, we may eventually develop a weekly news program from Washington, D.C.

One great burden on my heart is to establish a nationwide network of pregnancy crisis centers for unwed mothers. We must give these women an alternative to killing their unborn children. In our crisis centers, we will provide counseling, educational training, and adoption opportunities. Plenty of decent couples are unable to have children. Let them adopt the children of these unwed mothers. But don't kill the babies!

Another goal I have is the establishment of a Spanish division of CWA. When I was at the National Religious Broadcasters Convention in January 1984, three separate Spanish Christian leaders told me that more than one million Spanish-speaking women live in the state of New York, yet only the liberals have a strong influence on them. These Christian leaders have offered to help me reach out to this vast population, not only in New York but also all over America. Eventually we will have a Spanish edition of our CWA newsletter and our seminars will be interpreted for the Spanish as well.

What has been going on in Maryland with state director Mary Jane Wright is indicative of what we will be able to accomplish in every state once we have trained leaders. Mary Jane took over as our state director in the summer of 1980, not long after CWA was incorporated. Tim and I first met her when she drove us from the airport to our speaking engagement. As we talked, it became obvious to me that all three of us were on the same wavelength: we thought the same way, we had the same burdens for our nation. She joined CWA not long after that and volunteered to serve as our *first* state director.

Since then, Mary Jane Wright has organized and trained an army of committed Christian women to help her monitor the activities of the Maryland state legislature. She even has a lobbyist who testifies at hearings on issues of concern to CWA.

She and her friends have been active in pushing for tough anti-crime legislation. They have been successful in preventing a rise in state-funded abortions; they have helped to get a public display law passed, which requires that pornographic magazines not be displayed where children can see them.

She has also encouraged CWA members to become involved on the local level, donating their time for charitable activities—visiting the poor, ministering to prisoners. One of her state board members has opened a pregnancy crisis center to minister to the emotional and spiritual needs of unwed mothers.

I am praying that what she has accomplished in

Chapter 15

GOD'S CHALLENGE TO WOMEN

As I have gone over the brief history of our women's organization, I have been thrilled to see all that God has accomplished in such a short time span. In five years, we have grown from a handful of women to many hundreds of thousands. Our numerical growth has been phenomenal, but our pro-family activities and victories have been even more astounding.

I know the Lord has ordained CWA for an important function during these troubled times. We are awakening thousands of women to their responsibilities as citizens in this country. We are providing leadership and guidance for them in their numerous grassroots activities.

I believe, as I have stated before, that we Christian women were asleep too long. We focused solely on our families and church activities while the rest of our society was sliding into moral chaos. We ignored our schools, our government, our entertainment industry, our news media, and we've been paying a terrible price for our ignorance and apathy.

But the times are changing. We are here to keep the traditional women of America informed about the threats to the family. We're here to defend the religious liberties of those who fall victim to the humanist attack.

We have become a Christian women's alternative to feminism. In addition, we're here to pray for our leaders and to be a powerful influence for good in Washington, D.C.

In the early years of CWA, the Lord quickened a passage to me from Ephesians 5:11-14. I read,

> Have nothing to do with the fruitless deeds of darkness, but rather expose them. For it is shameful even to mention what the disobedient do in secret. But everything exposed by the light becomes visible, for it is light that makes everything visible. This is why it is said: "Wake up, O sleeper, rise from the dead, and Christ will shine on you."

Every one of those verses had special meaning for me. I knew that I was not having anything to do with the works of darkness. But those verses demanded much more of me than simply abstaining from sin. I was called to expose sin wherever I found it.

I was to be active, alert, and vigilant in the pursuit of personal holiness. I and so many thousands of other women had been asleep for too long. I was to wake up, and then Christ would shine upon the works He had given me to do.

That is the call to every Christian woman today: to be holy, alert, and active. We are to bear fruit in every good work, whether it is working in an orphanage or working to get tough antipornography legislation enforced in a community.

I have also taken as my own another verse: "You are the salt of the earth. But if the salt loses its saltiness, how can it be made salty again? It is no longer good for anything, except to be thrown out and trampled by men" (Matt. 5:13).

Jesus' words apply to all of us who claim to be His followers. What does it mean to be salt? If you think about salt's purpose, the meaning will become clearer. Salt in food serves as a seasoning to make the food taste better. It influences the food, improving its flavor.

Christians are to be salt in the society in which they live. They are to season the culture, improving it through their lives and actions.

Salt is also a preservative. Meat packed in salt will last a long time. We Christians are to be a preserving influence in our society. We are to protect traditional morality and uphold justice for everyone. We are to be model citizens. And this means we are going to be called upon at some time in our lives to stand up against unrighteousness. We are going to have to be willing to put our lives on the line if need be.

Salt is also a mineral used to heal wounds and cleanse infections. Looking around our society, it should be obvious to us that we are living in a spiritually and emotionally sick environment. Sexual perversions are now flaunted in public by mass political movements. We have millions of teen-agers who have destroyed their minds on drugs; we have suicides, teen pregnancies, abortion, and pornography. Adultery and alcoholic drinks are glorified on television and in the movies. Crime and fear have pervaded our land.

As the salt of the earth, we are to be here to heal the wounds of those who have been victimized by the purveyors of moral filth and permissiveness. We are here to offer healing to our land of its sins against God. We are to act, so God's promise in 2 Chronicles 7:14 can become a reality: "If my people, who are called by my name, will humble themselves and pray and seek my face and turn from their wicked ways, then will I hear from heaven and will forgive their sin and will heal their land."

The Lord is speaking to all believers in Jesus Christ. He's not talking to those who don't yet know the Lord. He is telling us in this verse that we have an awesome responsibility. He has given us this unconditional promise: if we will confess our sins, get our own lives straightened out, and pray to Him for deliverance, God will not only forgive us of our personal sins but will also cleanse and restore our land.

That is the challenge that lies ahead for Concerned Women for America. We are called by God to be a powerful influence in America for righteousness. But we must be right with God before He will empower us for this work.

I invite you to join with us in one of the most important women's movements in the history of this nation—or for that matter—the entire world. The women of Brazil took a stand for righteousness, and they saved their nation from a communist revolution. Likewise, in America, women like Carolyn Grove, Vicki Frost, Suzanne Clark and others have taken their stand for righteousness against the tyranny of secular humanism. This may be the year that God uses the organized prayers and action of thousands of Christian women to turn this nation around—to halt the advance of feminism and humanism and the secularization of our culture.

Let me leave you with a final thought and a challenge from the Word of God. In Ephesians 5:15-16, we read, "Be very careful, then, how you live—not as unwise but as wise, making the most of every opportunity, because the days are evil."

If our personal freedoms are destroyed in this nation, the entire world will suffer. If America ever falls under the total control of the feminists and humanists, religious liberty will be snuffed out. We cannot allow this to happen.

We are living in dangerous, but exciting times. While there is still liberty, while we still have the freedom to pray and act and vote, let us be wise. Let us make the most of every opportunity. The days are evil, but you and I can stand for righteousness against the oncoming darkness.

If we are truly committed to Jesus Christ, we have no other alternative but to wage warfare against those who would destroy our children, our families, our religious liberties. There is no other option.

Notes

Chapter 1

1. Clarence W. Hall, "The Country That Saved Itself," *Reader's Digest* (November 1964), p. 143.
2. Ibid.
3. Ibid., p. 147.

Chapter 2

1. Daisy Hepburn, *Why Doesn't Somebody Do Something?* (Wheaton, Ill: Victor Books, 1980), p. 42.
2. Ibid., p. 50.
3. From a 1981 Christian Broadcasting Network documentary entitled "Xpose." Mrs. Heinrich was interviewed by producer Charles McCally for the segment on child pornography.

Chapter 3

1. "California Testimony from Mrs. Mary Schmitz before the Congressional Ad Hoc Committee Investigating the International Women's Year," Women Volunteers in Politics, P.O. Box 1073, National City, CA 92050.

Chapter 4

1. Betty Friedan, *It Changed My Life* (New York: Random House, 1976), p. 345.
2. *Women Of The Whole World*, No. 2, 1978.
3. *Toward World Understanding* (Book V, UNESCO, 1949), p. 58.
4. Ibid.

5. Rosemary Thomson, "Suffer Little Children...To Come Unto The Federal Government," (Good News Broadcasters, 1979), p. 4.

6. Ibid., p. 5.

7. Senator Orrin Hatch, *Congressional Record* (March 26, 1979).

8. Ibid.

Chapter 5

1. *Human Events* (February 16, 1980).

2. Ibid.

3. *Christian Life* (February 1980).

4. CWA Newsletter (February 1980), p. 2.

5. CWA Newsletter (March 1980), p. 3.

6. "White House Conference Shapes Up As Gay Affair," *Human Events* (February 16, 1980), p. 139.

7. *Christian Life* (February 1980).

Chapter 6

1. *The Library of Congress Congressional Research Bulletin No. HQ 1428, U.S.D.* Senate debate on ERA.

2. Senator Orrin G. Hatch, *The Equal Rights Amendment— Myths and Realities* (Savant Press, 1983), p. 59.

3. Ibid., p. 53.

4. *The Yale Law Journal* (Vol. 80, No. 5, 1971), p. 973.

5. *Legal Intelligencer* (August 24, 1977, Philadelphia County Court C. P. 1977).

6. 456 Pennsylvania 536, 318 A. 2d 324, 1974.

7. Sylvia Porter's Financial Column (April 9, 1975).

8. *The Library of Congress Congressional Research Bulletin No. HQ 1428, U.S.D.* Senate debate on ERA.

9. Beverly LaHaye, *I Am a Woman by God's Design* (Old Tappan, NJ: Fleming H. Revell, 1980), p. 132.

10. Karl Marx, *Economic Politique et Philosophie*, Vol. 1, pp. 38-40.

11. Gloria Steinem, *Saturady Review of Education* (March 1973).

12. *The Document: Declaration of Feminism*, pp. 1-2.

13. Ibid., p. 9.

14. "Struggle to End Sex Bias" (New York, The New York Chapter of NOW).

Chapter 8

1. John Dunphy, "A Religion for a New Age," *Humanist* (January/February 1983), p. 26.

Chapter 9

1. Suzanne Clark, "So Much for Innocence: The Evils of the NEA," *Bristol Herald Courier* (Sunday, January 24, 1982).
2. Ibid.
3. Ibid.
4. Ibid.
5. *Combatting the New Right*. A workbook published by the Western States Regional Staff of the National Education Association, p. 3.
6. Ibid., p. 21.

Chapter 10

1. Information on Carolyn Grove and *The Learning Tree* incident was obtained in an interview with Carolyn Grove conducted by the author.
2. Carolyn Grove interview.
3. Information on Vicki Frost and the textbook incident was obtained in part from an interview with Vicki Frost conducted by the author.
4. Vicki Frost interview.
5. Vicki Frost interview.

Chapter 11

1. *America—Great Crises In Our History Told By Its Makers* (Chicago, Ill: Veterans Of Foreign Wars, 1925), pp. 223-224.
2. Rus Walton, *One Nation Under God* (Washington, D.C.: Third Century Publishers, 1975), p. 33.

About the Author

Beverly LaHaye is president and founder of Concerned Women for America, a lecturer on family issues, and a radio and television co-host with her husband, Tim La-Haye. She has written six previous books. She is a member of the Council on National Policy and for five consecutive years has been named by Conservative Digest as one of the Ten Most Admired Conservative Non-Congressional Women in the United States.